WHO GIVES A DAM?

COLONEL JOHN PENNYCUICK C.S.I. AND THE PERIYAR PROJECT

By Matthew Sleap

Chennai • Bangalore

CLEVER FOX PUBLISHING
Chennai, India

Published by CLEVER FOX PUBLISHING 2025
Copyright © Matthew Sleap 2025

All Rights Reserved.
ISBN: 978-93-67077-21-4

This book has been published with all reasonable efforts taken to make the material error-free after the consent of the author. No part of this book shall be used, reproduced in any manner whatsoever without written permission from the author, except in the case of brief quotations embodied in critical articles and reviews.

The Author of this book is solely responsible and liable for its content including but not limited to the views, representations, descriptions, statements, information, opinions and references ["Content"]. The Content of this book shall not constitute or be construed or deemed to reflect the opinion or expression of the Publisher or Editor. Neither the Publisher nor Editor endorse or approve the Content of this book or guarantee the reliability, accuracy or completeness of the Content published herein and do not make any representations or warranties of any kind, express or implied, including but not limited to the implied warranties of merchantability, fitness for a particular purpose. The Publisher and Editor shall not be liable whatsoever for any errors, omissions, whether such errors or omissions result from negligence, accident, or any other cause or claims for loss or damages of any kind, including without limitation, indirect or consequential loss or damage arising out of use, inability to use, or about the reliability, accuracy or sufficiency of the information contained in this book.

CONTENTS

Table of Figures, Photographs and Maps .... *vii*
Acknowledgements .... *xi*
Preface .... *xiii*

1. Who Gives A Dam?: Colonel John Pennycuick and The Periyar Project 1
    Introduction 2

2. The Periyar Project 12
    The Periyar Dam 12
    The Scope of the Periyar Project 14
    The Geographical Context 14
    Historical Record of the Periyar Project 15

3. The Irrigation Legacy of Madura 18
    The Agricultural State of Madura 18
    Reconnaissance of the Western Ghats 19

4. Shaping the Enterprise 22
    Realising the Possibilities 22
    Vision of Potential 22
    Descent into Famine 25
    Hope for Irrigation 27

5. Victorian Planning 31
Preparation and Planning 31
The Logistic Challenge 33
Planning the Supply Lines 34
Manpower 35
The Interlocking System 36
The Final Plans Vision 38

6. Engagement with the Periyar River 41
The Tiger in the Periyar 41
Second Season Shock 41
Breaking the *impasse* of the Chasm 43
The Third Season 45
Keeping the Tiger at bay 48
Dual System of Vents and Byewash 51
Taming the Tiger in the Fifth Season 56
Dash for Destination in the Sixth Season 58
A Permanent Vent for Victory 60
Epidemic In the Seventh Season 61
A Convenient Respite from Surges and Disease 63
Tunnelling through the Western Ghats 64
Flanking Dams 66
The Grand Opening 67
Reporting Completion of Construction 69

7. Baptism from the Ghats 70
Irrigation Infrastructure 70
Intended Impact of Periyar Water 72
The Consequences of the Periyar Project 73

8. Agricultural Awakening 74
Technical Hitches 74
Vested Interests 74
Cultural Change 75
Agricultural Revolution 76

9. Model for Climate Emergency 78
Green Revolution 78
The Periyar Project today 78
Opportunities for the future 79

10. Cameo of a Leader – Colonel John Pennycuick 81
John Pennycuick – Record and Reputation 82
Family background and Early Life in India 83
Education 83
India Posting 84
The Abyssinia Campaign 85
Family Life 86
Character of A Leader 89

TABLE OF FIGURES, PHOTOGRAPHS AND MAPS

Figure 1. The Periyar Dam under construction c 1894 1

Figure 2. Aerial View of the Periyar Dam 12

Figure 3. Diagram of the Vaigai and Periyar rivers 15

Figure 4. Network of canals and tanks in Madura District..... 18

Figure 5. Diagram to show the location of the original and subsequent sites of the dam and the watershed crossing.......... 23

Figure 6. John Pennycuick's Sketch Map for relocating the site of the Periyar Dam 24

Figure 7. Famine in the Madras Presidency 1876-8 after the British School.. 26

Figure 8. Cross section of the Periyar River showing the proposed dimensions of a Dam 32

Figure 9. Section of the Watershed showing the Tunnel......... 33

Figure 10. Establishing supply lines from Lower Camp to the Periyar Dam Headworks.. 35

Figure 11. Recruiting Local Workers for the Periyar Project 36

Figure 12. Diagram of the proposed Layout of the Periyar Dam 38

Figure 13. Establishment of secure foundations by the deployment of wooden trestles 44

Figure 14. Early photograph of the Periyar Dam showing foundation Outline (flow from the left) 45

Figure 15. Closing the Front Wall of the Main Dam 46

Figure 16. Diagram of the Front and Rear of the Main Dam 47

Figure 17. Periyar River in flood over Main Dam Foundations 48

Figure 18. Right Bank Byewash Upscaling - first Byewash Diversion 52

Figure 19. Periyar Dam showing byewash upscaling to second line of piers 53

Figure 20. Temporary Vent development as dam height increases 54

Figure 21. Weir number 3 breached interrupting supplies 55

Figure 22. Main Dam Front Wall Elevated towards 37' 57

Figure 23. Filling in Temporary Vents 59

Figure 24. Number 2 Weir becomes the point from which material sent to the Main Dam 60

Figure 25. Permanent Vent Design 61

Figure 26. Increasing Proportion of workers reporting sick 62

Figure 27. Main Dam front and back wall development accelerating 64

Figure 28. Sluice Gates into the Tunnel 65

Figure 29. Watershed Cutting 66

Figure 30. Main and flanking Dams development from upstream 67

Figure 31. Opening Ceremony of the Periyar Project 68
Figure 32. Lord Wenlock and Project Staff 69
Figure 33. Network of canals for irrigation from
"the Periyar Project" 70
Figure 34. John Pennycuick probably taken in 1870.............. 81
Figure 35. Grace Pennycuick 87
Figure 36. Author at Memorial for John Pennycuick
at Lower Camp 91
Figure 37. The bust of John Pennycuick in the Memorial
Gardens, St Peter's Church, Frimley Parish presented by
Dr. A. K. Viswanathan, IPS 2018 92
Figure 38. Bust of John Pennycuick presented by the
Chief Minister of Tamil Nadu: M K Stalin 93

ACKNOWLEDGEMENTS

I would like to acknowledge and thank Stuart Sampson, great grandson of Colonel John Pennycuick who made the original letters and photographs available for this account of the Periyar Project and who has provided advice and guidance throughout. In particular he has taken the trouble to digitise the material so that it can be used to the benefit of understanding the extent of the endeavour involved in the development of the Periyar Project.

My thanks to Mark McConnell, whose great-grandfather on his mother's side, was Colonel John Pennycuick. Mark's meticulously researched family history has a beautifully written account of the life of Colonel John Pennycuick and the genealogical context for his celebrated endeavours in southern India.

Thanks to David and Ally Rivers for reviewing an early version of "Who Gives A Dam?" for engineering integrity and people aspects.

Thanks to Sue Ferro who took photographs of the Periyar Dam which illustrate the Dam close up from the reservoir perspective.

Thank you Santhana Beer oli for bringing the deeds and reputation of Colonel John Pennycuick to our attention in Camberley.

Thank you to my wife, Jane, for proof reading a series of drafts and travelling to India, and the Vrynwy Dam in Wales to research the background.

Thanks to Sally Kettle for proof reading an early version of the pamphlet intended for the inauguration of the statue in Camberley recreation centre.

I would also like to acknowledge the tribute given to John Pennycuick by the Member of Parliament for Surrey Heath, The Right Honourable Dr Al Pinkerton on the occasion of his maiden speech to the House of Commons in July 2024.

PREFACE

If it hadn't been for a congregant member of Frimley Parish near Camberley recognising the grave of Colonel John Pennycuick, we may never have delved into his background to understand the significance of his legacy. Santhana Beer oli from Theni District in Tamil Nadu revealed his personality to the people of Camberley as a man of great interest in the State of Tamil Nadu in southern India.

The entry for John Pennycuick in Who Was Who in India makes no mention of the Project he is associated with in India. His entry as Chief Engineer and Secretary to the Government in the Public Works and Marine Department refers rather to his cricketing skill and achievements.

As a result of the interest shown by the Tamil community of UK, John Pennycuick's great grandson, Stuart Sampson, generously released photographic records of the construction of the Periyar Project and letters between the officers engaged in the enterprise.

The insight these records afforded, in conjunction with a detailed engineering record, has enabled the author to piece together the narrative of the Project, the focus for which was construction of a dam and watershed crossing of the Western Ghats in southern India. The impact of the integration of the dam system on the vast and ancient hydrological system of the

District of Madura transformed the region in terms of the human way of life.

This transformation explains, in part, the admiration which persists in memory of John Pennycuick. The enduring respect and affection for his memory is also attributed to the way the Project was delivered, which is why this account of the Periyar Project is important. Dismissed as unachievable in 1800, the relentless pursuit of a feasible approach for connecting the District of Madura to a region of bountiful water was led by John Pennycuick as a junior officer. Delivery of the Project was stalked by failure over eight years despite meticulous planning but John Pennycuick's ingenuity and imaginative application of engineering techniques succeeded in the mission through a coordinated effort by workers and engineers from across the region.

John Pennycuick succeeded in more than transforming the agro-economy. He empowered the community to change their way of life and exploit the new found opportunity to become entrepreneurs which is why his iconic image can be seen on the entrance to smallholdings and market gardens between Madurai and Thekkady today.

Whilst the engineering community was engaged in the technical innovations of the engineering aspects of the Project, which John Pennycuick subsequently presented to the Institute of Civil Engineers, the human impact was first reported by the Royal Geographical Society in 1895, the year of the completion of the project. The prosperity of the region today can be linked with the aspirations and opportunities made real by the Periyar Project. The appreciation shown by the people of Tamil Nadu for the life and works of John Pennycuick is something to be cherished and nurtured both in India and in the UK.

This book describes the Periyar Project and the endeavour led by Colonel John Pennycuick, and the impact of the Project on the population of the Vaigai Valley of Tamil Nadu.

WHO GIVES A DAM?[1]: COLONEL JOHN PENNYCUICK AND THE PERIYAR PROJECT

Figure 1. The Periyar Dam under construction c 1894

---

[1]According to Sathnam Sanghera, in Empireland, "Dam" originally referred to a copper coin, for example, "the fortieth part of a rupee" and so low in value that it led to Britons in India employing the phrase "I won't give a Dumri", which led in turn to the popular expression "I don't give a dam(n)."

Introduction

Our relationship with the British Empire is often associated with struggle for power and anarchy often discussed as a legacy of shame. In the case of India, the correction to the influence of the East India Company by the introduction of direct rule from Britain, introduced changes to the administration and offered greater opportunities to indigenous people. The Indian Civil Service introduced greater local representation and opportunities for advancement.

Whilst railways and infrastructure projects were joining up the Indian subcontinent, the situation for most people was not improving. Indeed, for some, particularly in southern India, it was in decline and the future only seemed to be one of marginalisation.

It was into this context that John Pennycuick was posted to the Madras Engineering Group as a young subaltern from his officer training course at Addiscombe College, England, in 1860. The area of his posting in India, though remote from the centre of administration and government in Calcutta, was blessed with a military and civil administration in Madras and Bangalore that delivered great engineering works to improve the way of life of the local communities and the environment. The Madras Engineering Group's area of responsibility was large and diverse in terms of both geography and people covering much of southern India except for Princely States including Travancore.

John Pennycuick identified himself with the struggle for survival of the people of a culturally distinct area of India in the far southern part of the Madras Engineering Group area of responsibility. The district of Madura and the Vaigai

Valley is geographically defined by a vast and ancient irrigation network focused on the trading city of Madurai with a history of managing a thriving economy. Changes in the balance of nature and the climate brought increasing hardship and poverty through calamitous drought in the 19th Century which became progressively more damaging. The once thriving Ramnad dynasty faced with an existential threat to its people and economy was in apparently hopeless decline. Farmers and artisans were emigrating from the region. There were persistent urgent appeals from the local communities to the Madras Engineering Group to help exploit the plentiful resource of water from the Periyar River in the Western Ghats to alleviate water shortage.

John Pennycuick and the Periyar Project are inextricably linked not only because the major part of his career as an engineer officer was to deliver a solution to this parlous situation, but also because destiny landed him with a calling.

The subaltern officer, John Pennycuick became inalienably associated with the Peryiar Project when he had to take responsibility for the results of the reconnaissance of the Western Ghats by Major Ryves in 1869. The valiant odyssey by Major Ryves over several seasons sought a solution to an economic and cultural crisis that the population of Madura had invested in through an irrigation network of vast proportion. Although Major Ryves' proposal was technically unfeasible, there was sufficient plausibility in his approach to warrant further investigation. John Pennycuick with his technical qualification from Addiscombe College, his experience from the Abyssinian campaign and sensing a challenge, if not a moral crusade was captivated and recruited support from

Mr Smith of the Indian Civil Service for a submission to the Madras Engineering Group of a solution for the crisis.

Campaign hardened John Pennycuick was peculiarly well equipped for the challenge of using the experience handed to him by Ryves. His deployment with the Madras Engineering Group on the Abyssinia Campaign in 1867 enhanced its capability to undertake a large scale enterprise making use of tested innovation from the campaign. John Pennycuick's deployment on that campaign as H Troop Commander gave him leadership experience. He engaged in the building of road, railways, bridges and projecting communications and logistics over large distances in rugged terrain and high relief. He was awarded a campaign medal and Mention in Despatches.

The Periyar Project in it's fullest extent became his sole responsibility from 1882 when he became the Chief Engineer of the Periyar Project. The development of the Periyar dam became the key component without which none of the other aspects would work to deliver the transformation of peoples' way of life. Logistically remote, in a hazardous environment, employing new technology on a scale that exceeded the Vrynwy Dam[2] in Wales, implementation of a dam was dangerous and carried a high risk.

He had been helped in this endeavour by the Public Works Department and Madras Engineering Group. A survey conducted in the 1870's of the Periyar Project showed the full potential impact of water availability on existing irrigation works would make at least 150,000 acres of land amenable to cultivation compared

---

[2] The experience of other similar masonry dam projects at St Etienne in France and Suez and Aswan dams in Egypt were unavailable to the engineers of the Periyar Project.

to 20,000 acres under cultivation at the time. The extent of the historic canal system and local hydrological experience showed that the population was committed to make use of the water from such a Project. A financial assessment based on the survey by Mr Clougsden of the Public Works Department in 1876 clearly identified the financial viability of a such a Project.

The tragedy of the southern Indian famine of 1876 to 1879 was the sad and clinching argument for the need for the Periyar Project. The remoteness of the region from the centre of government in Calcutta, poor communications and sheer scale of the famine was recounted by the Viceroy's envoy for famine, Sir Richard Temple, who toured the region and kept a journal that likened the devastation to a war. As news of the famine became clear in London, the issue was debated in Parliament which voted for famine relief and, crucially, longer term measures to improve the economy. Florence Nightingale tabled changes that covered technical, economic and political proposals which had at their core improved resilience of the water supply.

A mysterious delay to the authorisation for the Project to proceed following approval of a masonry dam occurred after John Pennycuick was appointed as Chief Engineer of the Periyar Project in 1882. It may have been because funds previously allocated to large engineering projects were diverted to famine relief and measures necessary to improve the welfare of the community. There are, however, references in the engineering report and in correspondence that the development of the Vrynwy Dam in Wales, the first masonry dam in Britain, was being observed as a pathfinder project for the Periyar Project dam construction.

The design of the Vrynwy Dam was using the same engineering innovative principle as John Pennycuick was proposing for the Periyar Project. John Pennycuick did indeed return to Britain, ostensibly to procure logistic supplies but possibly also to review progress on the Vrynwy project. In any event, John Pennycuick was given the approval to proceed with urgency in 1887.

Projecting the engineering capability and logistic support to carry out the enterprise at the dam site over distance and terrain benefitted from John Pennycuick's deployment on the Abyssinian campaign. There is no doubt that he learnt daring and adaptability during his deployment on the Abyssinian Campaign which was invaluable experience. He applied this experience to the Periyar dam site, 8 miles from the nearest road and up a scarp face of nearly 2,000 feet cloaked in forest where the headworks for the operation had to be established and functioning and the manpower organised for the construction operation to commence.

The combination of wire ropeways, railways, canals and a metalled road were considered to project heavy lifting capability to complement the cart tracks from the road at Lower Camp, the bottom of the Ghaut scarp. A settlement at Thekkady near the watershed ridge line was established to administer a workforce that would, at times, number 6,000.

Projecting capability was only part of the challenge. The workforce had to employ a great range of skills and it was the responsibility of the Officer Ernest Logan to recruit, hire and manage the men coming from diverse geographic areas. Some local labour from Cumbum in the Vaigai Valley, was employed on piece work terms but this was unpopular and anyway, the people returned to the village at harvest time when they were most needed at the dam headworks. The cities of Madurai and Coimbatore provided masons and carpenters were recruited from the west coast near Cochi. Drillers for quarrying work were generally available and easily taught the use of the machinery. But the vast majority of the labour force was from far and wide and the turnover high. Labour relations were at times strained but the high incidence of disease which constrained operations to a season between June and March of the following year was a limitation on the development of the dam that reduced productivity. In the final year of construction of the dam, an outbreak of cholera brought operations to a complete halt and forced the team to relocate the labourers' accommodation to the south side of the river. This terrible tragedy blighted the final stage of the Periyar Project.

The energy in the Periyar River is analogous to the savage muscle power of a tiger. Taming the tiger energy of the Periyar River to build a dam was treacherous, ambushing each planned initiative with violence so intense that three additional seasons were needed beyond the five that were originally funded to control the dynamics of the river. The Project team failed to identify a great chasm in the riverbed that would stymie progress for the greater part of the first season. Surges, locally referred to as "freshes" in the river initiated high in the Western Ghats arrived at the dam headworks without warning but with such speed and force that the river would typically rise fifteen feet in less than three hours bearing great tree trunks and rolling rocks measured in tons against the nascent dam.

Time and again, the operational response to these crises was led by John Pennycuick with a team of dedicated engineer officers whose loyalty and commitment was exemplary. But it was John Pennycuick whose initiatives would save the day and whose sure-footed engineering established the resilience of the vulnerable structure that was first established in 1888. His initiative to secure the chasm in the river with wooden trestles filled and secured with ground rock established a bulwark and a bridge across the river for establishing foundations. His insistence on using open vents during construction of the main dam avoided certain destruction in the early stages. A permanent vent established after the front wall was of sufficient height to withstand surges then served to control the level of the water until completion of the project.

The tunnel was begun and drilled concurrently with the main dam project, but progress was slow through the granite rock. John Pennycuick led and inspired by example, demonstrating how a straight line could be plotted for the tunnel across the seven summits of the Western Ghats using new instruments. A vertical shaft was sunk at about the midway point of the projected tunnel to create a second drill face in the opposite direction to accelerate the pace of development. The tunnels met in October 1894 with extraordinary accuracy and the whole tunnel was completed with a sluice early in 1895. The sluice was designed to regulate the flow of water into the Vaigai Valley so that there was always water available in the reservoir for irrigation. During the first year of operation, the sluice failed during the driest part of the year preventing water being held back and therefore unavailable for irrigation. The sluice was replaced and subsequently successfully controlled the delivery of water throughout the year into the Vaigai Valley.

The watershed cutting was the link between the sill of the reservoir and the sluice gate into the tunnel. A canal had to be dug from the sluice gate using local labour until the necessary fall of ground was sufficient to reverse the flow of the Muliar Panjan tributary. Until that time, the Muliar Panjan tributary was to be used as a canal to transport heavy materials. An initial lock system to control water depth in the Muliar Panjan was abandoned in favour of three weirs where the heavy materials would have to be transhipped by a complex crane and chute mechanism. This was frequently disrupted and eventually abandoned after surges travelled up to the third weir and deposited huge tree trunks in the way of barges. Eventually sufficient depth of the watershed cutting was achieved with revetting of the banks to reverse the flow into the sluice gates in time for the inauguration of the dam.

Coordination of the completion of the flanking right bank Spillway and the left bank Baby Dam was necessary to coincide with the completion of the main dam. John Pennycuick delegated responsibility for implementing these critical aspects of the project. Survey exposed difficulties with the geology of the natural depressions in the bedrock. The Right Bank Spillway used a rocky spur to provide a firm foundation. The left bank Baby Dam development could not find firm bedrock for a masonry dam extension except for a very short distance from the main dam. An earthen dam extension was used to complete the construction. The flanking dams were therefore completed to coincide with the main dam completion.

The opening ceremony for the inauguration for the diversion of water into the Vaigai valley was presided over by Lord Wenlock, Governor of Madras but was as much a political act as ceremonial because it was attended by the Bishop of Travancore, the Princely

State through which the Periyar River flowed. The land for the reservoir and dam had been leased from Travancore for 999 years.

The impact of the Periyar Project was immediate, progressive and persists to current times. The overarching result was that the Project worked immediately. The area of land under irrigation increased to 50,000 acres. A second crop was realised in the same year over a proportion of the land dedicated to the first crop led by the zamindari landlords who set the example for ryot farmers to follow. The extent and intensity of irrigation in the Vaigai Valley increased in following years in line with projections made by the Project.

There were significant issues to overcome which needed intervention by government. Where vested interests of the zaminderi landlords were threatened, they would block supplies to the ryot farmers. The Irrigation Act was brought into law to protect the access of ryot farmers to publicly owned irrigation for the community. The availability of water meant that farmers would need to reschedule sowing to take full advantage of the availability of water which would take time and re-education by the Madras Government. The extension of irrigation to new, relatively dry lands required fertiliser which was unavailable locally. The government provided loans to ryot farmers who were unable to procure appropriate fertiliser for their land. These changes brought about the general transition to a market economy that would significantly improve the way of life of the farmers of the Vaigai Valley. The opportunities for this economic transformation could only come about through the availability of Periyar water.

The opportunities presented to the region are associated with John Pennycuick to this day. His spirit of endeavour seems to have captured the affection and admiration particularly of small holder farmers and market gardeners who make a business out of growing a range of crops. Their entrepreneurship has been facilitated by the availability of a reliable water supply. But the recognition of this achievement has spread to the civic level with presentation of a bust of John Pennycuick and a plinth for the grave in his burial place at St Peter's Church, Frimley by the then Commissioner of Police, Dr. A. K. Viswanathan, IPS in 2018. This was followed by a bust in Camberley Town centre presented by Tamil Nadu Chief Minister, Mr M K Stalin in 2022.

It was the courage and conviction of John Pennycuick that drove the Periyar Project. Imperilled by seemingly insuperable issues on a number of occasions, John Pennycuick could respond with unorthodox but effective techniques and approaches. His attitude is a model for the climate emergency we face in the 21st Century. Undoubtedly, he would be considering how the Periyar Project could contribute to providing renewable energy beyond the hydroelectric power generated at the water tunnel exit. He would be considering the opportunities available for solar energy from floating solar at the tanks and at the reservoir. But the requirements would be driven by the interests of local people to improve the environment and way of life.

THE PERIYAR PROJECT

The Periyar Dam

The Periyar Dam (sometimes referred to as the Mullaiperiyar Dam) is on a great scale, ranked with the oldest and grandest hydrological projects in the world[3]. The Periyar Main Dam is 155 feet high and a third of a mile long with, additionally, a separate spillway dam on the right bank and a baby dam on the left bank of the Periyar River spanning the Periyar valley. The flanking dams occupy natural depressions in the landscape and the spillway provides an escape whenever there is an excessive depth of water at the main dam. The extent of the dam and associated works is shown in the following diagram.

Figure 2. Aerial View of the Periyar Dam
Source: Earth View - Map 3D

---

[3]UNU-INWEH Report Series 11. Ageing Water Storage Infrastructure: An Emerging Global Risk

The Periyar Dam is only a part of The Periyar Project with much greater scope than the dam site, referred to as the Headworks during construction. The purpose of the Periyar Dam is to impound a reservoir an area of 8000 acres, almost twice the area of Lake Windermere in England, at a level that maintains a continuous controlled flow of water into a cutting and tunnel through the Western Ghats Mountains. The Periyar Dam started to turn water continuously from the Periyar River into the tunnel through the mountains from 1895.

The achievement was apparently first reported in Britain in the Monthly Record of the Royal Geographical Society at a meeting in December 1895 in terms of a diversion of the upper course of the Periyar River, southern India. The Report, giving credit to Colonel Pennycuick for the engineering achievement, anticipated the human benefit as "controlling the supply from the reservoir down to the valley of the Vaigai, into which the new supply is directed, as well as those for irrigation in the same valley, by which an area of 220 square miles in the Madura plain will be fertilized".

The Record reported that "the project had been considered at various times from 1808 onwards, but only put into execution in 1887 upon plans prepared by for diverting the upper course of the Periyar from its normal direction towards the west coast, and carrying it across the watershed via a canal and tunnel, to the opposite side of the peninsula, has lately been completed".

The Scope of the Periyar Project

The output of the tunnel from the reservoir connects with an ancient irrigation network of rivers and canals in the Vaigai Valley. The irrigation network was modernised as part of The Periyar Project to accept water from the reservoir and deliver a continuous, controlled and reliable flow through the irrigation network to farmers in the Vaigai Valley and beyond.

The Geographical Context

The Periyar River rises in the Western Ghats at an altitude of 1,830 m (6,000 feet) where there is a broad catchment exposed to the southwest monsoon. The average annual rainfall is 4,000 mm (156 inches) in the upstream catchment before being joined by the Mullayar River with a similarly large catchment. By the time the joint river water reaches the site of the dam, it has fallen almost 3,000 feet over a distance less than 20 miles and has great force. The rainfall tends to be concentrated during the southwest monsoon, arriving as sudden surges or "Freshes[4]" that can be frequent and considerable in volume and intensity. These events can be sudden, in clear skies and without warning at any time of year.

The Vaigai River by contrast flows east from the Western Ghats and after a short plunge down the scarp slope of less than 2,000 feet has a flat profile and is therefore slow-flowing until it reaches the sea in the Bay of Bengal. The Vaigai River is 258 kilometres (160 miles) long, with a drainage basin 7,031 square

---

[4]A term used throughout the documents and letters to refer to the sudden surges in the flow of the Periyar River and tributaries when monsoon rains occurred sometimes a long way upstream and out of sight of storm clouds that might herald heavy rain. Thus they could catch any labour force working on the river totally unawares.

kilometres (2,715 sq miles) large. Much of the upper reaches of the valley lie in the rainfall shadow of the Western Ghats and receive on average 33 inches of rain mostly during the northeast monsoon but this can be unreliable. The river water is widely distributed across the Vaigai valley by a traditional canal system.

The following map shows the Vaigai Valley in relation to the Periyar River and the watershed of the Western Ghats.

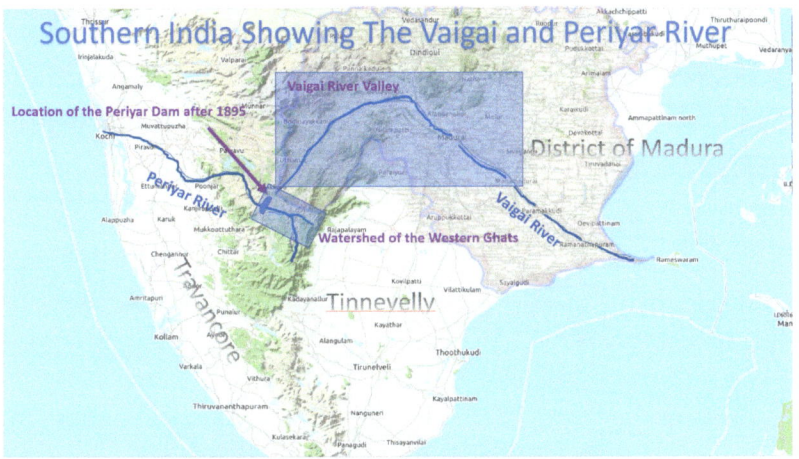

Figure 3. Diagram of the Vaigai and Periyar rivers
Source: Map data from OpenStreetMap

Historical Record of the Periyar Project

Much of what we know about the Periyar Project is derived from engineering documents written by A T Mackenzie, Executive Engineer of the Periyar Dam, including his report, "The History Of The Periyar Project". In addition, the Chief Engineer of The Periyar Project, Colonel John Pennycuick, delivered a documented presentation on the design and construction of the Periyar Dam to the Institute of Civil Engineers in London in 1897, two years after the completion of the Periyar Project. Both accounts attribute the success of the Project to Colonel John Pennycuick who assumed responsibility as Chief Engineer for design, planning and delivery of the project from 1882.

Colonel John Pennycuick's great grandson, Stuart Sampson, provided letters and photographs about the development of the Periyar Project. These documents together with the engineering report by A T Mackenzie provide insight into the challenges experienced in the development of the Project. An assessment of the Project was presented by Colonel John Pennycuick in person to the Institute of Civil Engineers on 26th January 1897 after his return to England. His co-presenter, Mr P R Allen, the engineer in charge of tunnelling, presented on the associated tunnel, and both presentations were accompanied by discussion and further correspondence by many leading engineers of the period.

By bringing together engineering documents written by A T Mackenzie, and Colonel John Pennycuick's presentation to the Institute of Civil Engineers, we now realise that the Project was an audacious enterprise in scale and technology, mounted in a remote region of India that would test to the limit the resourcefulness and innovation of the supporting organisation, the Public Works Department and the military formation responsible for delivering the project, the Madras Engineering Group.

The incentive for a project which carried such a high risk was derived from the impoverishment of a once flourishing economy around the city of Madurai and the governing Ramnad Dynasty. The fundamental problem was geographical orientation in that the area lies in the rain shadow of the Western Ghats and mountains that lie to the north that has periodically deprived the region of water from rainfall runoff leading to long periods of drought.

As Chief Engineer, Colonel John Pennycuick appreciated the situation of the people of the Vaigai Valley and Madura District and brought into being the concept behind the Periyar Project with great leadership and determination to deliver an enduring capability inaugurating a change to the way of life in the Taluks along the Vaigai River basin, particularly Madura.

THE IRRIGATION LEGACY OF MADURA

The Agricultural District of Madura

A water conservation system dating from the 10th Century had been developed for the District of Madura consisting of a network of canals, small dams (anicuts) and irrigation tanks. The system effectively captured the flow from the Vaigai River and associated tributaries for irrigation of the area around the regional capital of Madurai. This sophisticated system sustained an agricultural economy that flourished for millennia. Father Martin, a missionary who worked in Madura District, documented the existence of a hydrological network in 1713 that was later detailed in The Madura Manual by the government engineer, the Collector of Madura.

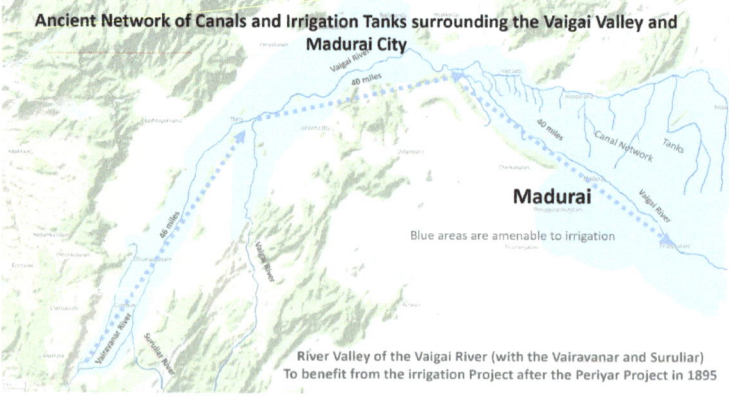

Figure 4. Network of canals and tanks in Madura District
Source: Map data from OpenStreetMap

Speculation about diverting water from the relatively moist west of India into the Vaigai Valley had preoccupied local governments since the existence of the canal network because increasing periods of drought depleted the water supplies. Rain-fed irrigation tanks around the canal network were developed for storage, but there was inadequate water supply to top them up even from the flow of the Vaigai River. The Collector of Madura presented a proposal to divert the Periyar River in 1808, which was dutifully investigated through a formal reconnaissance by Captain James Caldwell but was dismissed as unachievable.

Reconnaissance of the Western Ghats

Persistent and increasing drought over half a century prompted the Madras Engineering Group to re-examine the issue and despatch Major Ryves to make a detailed reconnaissance lasting until 1869 to re-examine the possibilities for new water supply. His long reconnaissance yielded plans and intelligence for the construction of a dam at a site where water could be turned across the watershed of the Western Ghats. Major Ryves' diligent survey provided detailed knowledge of the terrain and local conditions as well as the behaviour of the Periyar River. He identified possible sites for diverting the water across the watershed by understanding the differential relief of the river and the watershed for possible locations of an earthen dam.

The observations by Major Ryves over five years showed that the ferocity of surges or "Freshes", as they were known, would however, probably destroy an earthen dam. Nonetheless, he found a site where the Periyar River runs parallel to the watershed of the Western Ghats and a saddle or col in the ridge barely 200 feet above the river where a cutting could be achieved to divert water onto the eastern flank of the mountains.

Major Ryves made a blueprint for the construction of an earthen dam that would be high enough and impound sufficient water to cross the watershed but realised that the structure, needing to be 200 feet high, would have to be of completely different design and material to survive the surges during construction and impound a deep reservoir. His conclusion differed from previous expeditions, however, in that, given the appropriate technology, it would be possible to achieve the hitherto unachievable diversion and yield sufficient quantity of water to irrigate agricultural land in the Vaigai Valley.

This significant conclusion incentivised the Madras Engineering Group and John Pennyquick to continue the quest for a way of bringing a constant supply of water across the Western Ghats.

It appears that the then young Captain John Pennycuick met Major Ryves in a handover of responsibility between engineers that would inspire the young engineer to maintain the pursuit for a solution. Captain John Pennycuick had returned from the acclaimed Abyssinian Campaign in 1869 inspired with ideas gleaned from the many engineering achievements of that campaign and envisaged ways in which he could apply the experience to the engineering problem at hand.

Captain John Pennycuick, though not yet given authority for the Project, benefitted from the insight provided by Major Ryves' proposal to dam the Periyar River in a number of ways which was arguably the inspiration for his engineering approach. Firstly

Major Ryves warned about the environmental hazards of working in the forest of the Western Ghats. He himself had become ill from the fevers that were prevalent between the period of March and June of each year and this observation would dictate the working season for future projects. He also detailed an approach which would involve the building of coffer dams to stem the flow of the Periyar river during surges in the river level. He offered diagrams of how this could be achieved including the building of a byewash channel which could carry away excess water whilst staff continued to work in the cover of a cofferdam. These expedients, though theoretical at this stage, were to be invaluable to the construction of the dam at a later date.

The young Captain not only benefitted from the experience of Major Ryves but also the understanding of the Madras Engineering Group about southern India. The Madras Engineering Group was one of the few military organisations which survived the reforms of direct rule from Britain following the Sepoy Rebellion. The accumulated experience within the Group about southern Indian society spanning the East India Company rule gave the young captain great insight into the needs of the government and the difficulties of the agricultural economy. He had access to a trove of information to draw upon mainly in the gazettes published in the previous hundred years but particularly J H Nelson who authored The Madura Country in 1868

SHAPING THE ENTERPRISE

Realising the Possibilities

John Pennycuick engaged with the Periyar Project enthusiastically after his return to India following deployment on the Abyssinia Campaign in 1869. He made an appreciation of the plans submitted by Major Ryves and in conjunction with the then Chief Engineer of the Public Works Department, Mr Smith, recommended that the Periyar Dam had to be constructed as a masonry dam.

This decision may also have been informed by the innovative plans for the Vrynwy Dam in Wales which was the first masonry dam in Britain and to which there are references in the Project Report. It seems clear that John Pennycuick realised the potential of the plans submitted by Major Ryves but only with the strength that a masonry dam could provide. Moreover, the more robust construction of a masonry dam offered the opportunity to expand the scale of the dam and reservoir to support his vision.

Vision of Potential

As John Pennycuick made further reconnaissance of the Periyar River, following the handover from Major Ryves, he relocated the site of the dam in a decision that would have a profound impact on the outcome of the Project. He situated the new dam site 7 miles downstream of the site identified by Major Ryves thus increasing the potential capacity of the reservoir at least threefold.

This decision meant that sufficient water would be available to divert to the Vaigai valley with continuous uninterrupted flow throughout the year. The impact would be to allow farmers to plan to grow two crops each year in areas dependent on the irrigation system and to extend the area under irrigation from the increased volume of water from an enlarged reservoir.

The new site also provided an opportunity to create escapes for excess water in natural depressions either side of the Main Dam which would be necessary to control the considerable quantities of water impounded by the reservoir. The following diagram shows the Major Ryves proposed site and the chosen site of the Periyar Dam with the potential reservoir area including the proposed diversions across the Western Ghats

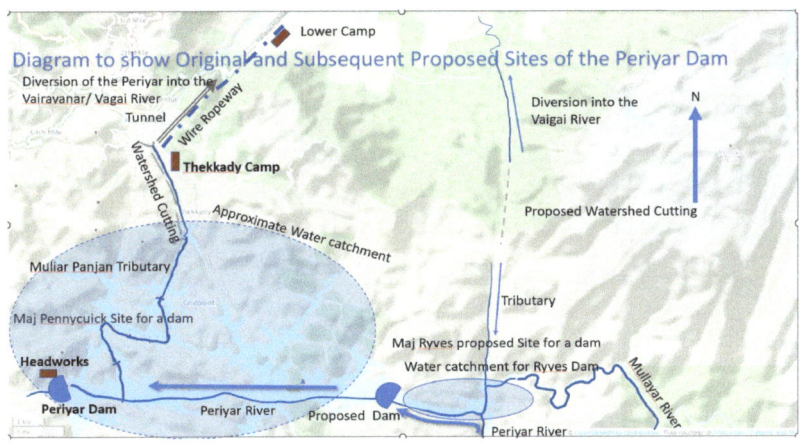

Figure 5. Diagram to show the location of the original and subsequent sites of the dam and the watershed crossing
Source: Map Data from OpenStreetMap

We know this revised strategy for siting the Dam strategy was at the instigation of John Pennycuick because he presented

Shaping the Enterprise

this idea using his own diagram to the Institute of Civil Engineers after his return to Britain in 1897 which is reproduced below. His sketch map shows the upper site, proposed by Major Ryves, and the lower actual site chosen with the routes to the watershed crossing for both options.

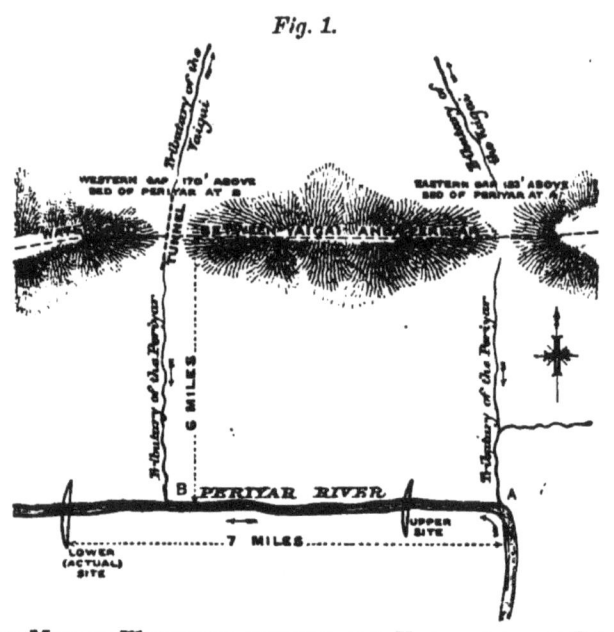

Figure 6. John Pennycuick's Sketch Map for relocating the site of the Periyar Dam

The new location for the Periyar Dam also required a different approach for diverting water from the reservoir that Major Ryves had recommended. Instead of an open cutting, the new approach involved cutting a tunnel over a mile long though the watershed of the Western Ghats which would regulate the flow of water into the Vaigai valley more precisely than an open aqueduct. This intent is also clearly shown on the diagram above with a tunnel indicated through the watershed.

The significance of this change meant that farmers in the Vaigai valley would have access to water throughout the year and the opportunity to irrigate a second crop. In addition, for the longer term, the Project could produce hydroelectricity. John Pennycuick claimed the credit for both these visionary changes in his presentation to the Institute of Civil Engineers in 1897.

These plans were presented for approval to the government by the Madras Engineering Group in 1872 but were stalled by the very condition they were intended to mitigate, the onset of drought across southern India resulting in widespread famine. This was because funding assigned to engineering projects had to be diverted to immediate famine relief.

Descent into Famine

Low agricultural productivity had affected Madura for years because of meagre rainfall resulting from the rain shadow effect of the Western Ghats, compounded by silting of the irrigation tanks which reduced the volume of water that could be held for irrigation. Drought regularly afflicted the Vaigai Valley, reducing agricultural productivity and impoverishing the community. The economic resilience of the community was progressively eroded, rendering them vulnerable to poverty and a state of hopeless dependency on the administration.

The Southern Indian Famine of 1876 - 9 devastated the already weakened agricultural community. Although few written records exist for events in the area, Sir Richard Temple, the Viceroy's envoy for famine districts in 1877, maintained a journal of his tour of affected districts. Sir Richard attributed the famine to the drought, characterising its progress through the southern Indian states as a marauding army. To quote his journal "it extended itself with havoc throughout the southern peninsula, laying waste the districts of Madura and Tinnevelly (the District to the south of Madura); all hope of the monsoon was given up".

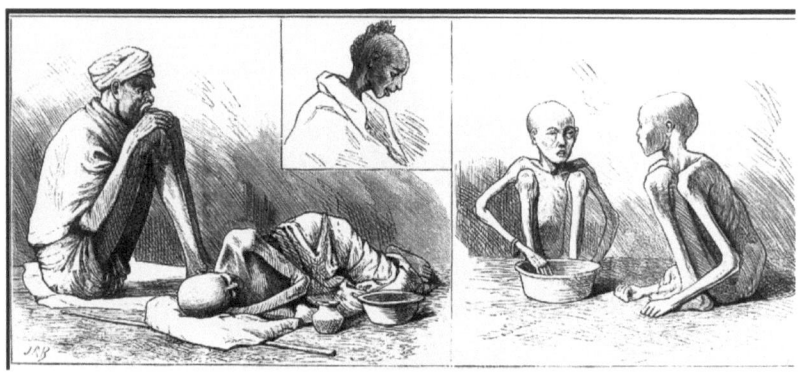

Figure 7. Famine in the Madras Presidency 1876-8 after the British School

Poor communications by road and rail meant that relief aid was slow to arrive, and mortality rates were consequently high.

This situation resulted in intense political pressure from Parliament in England not only to alleviate the suffering but to put in place long-term changes. Florence Nightingale, empowered by her influence through political connections, campaigned vigorously for the irrigation tanks to be refurbished so that they held more water. She recognised the importance of the existing canal and tank system not only for short term amelioration of drought but for the longer term she understood their importance to the agricultural system. Above all, a continuous source of water independent of runoff from the bi-annual monsoon was necessary to replenish the tanks and provide water for irrigation.

Hope for Irrigation

The Financial Director of the Madras Engineering Group, Mr Clogstoun, encouraged by the apparent feasibility of diverting waters from the Western Ghats, made an assessment of the financial viability of the Peryiar Project in 1876. His assessment made the assumption that the diverted water would be available to the entire network of rivers, canals, and water tanks lying mostly in the Theni, Dindigul (southern part) Melur and Madurai Taluks within the Madura District. He estimated that the potential cultivable area was approximately 150,000 acres. Much of the area was arable, and amenable to irrigation. This assumption, however, needed to be properly surveyed.

He conducted a detailed investigation that assessed the existing area of cultivated land that would benefit from the supply of water, including the potential of those areas for a second crop. Over 50% of the land was supplied by rain-fed tanks (75,878 acres), whilst only 5,000 acres was irrigated by anicut channels (1,000 acres) and Korambu[5] channels (4,000 acres). To this he added 15,210 acres of so-called "dry lands" under inam[6] and zamindari[7] control in villages, giving a total of 96,088 acres under cultivation that

---

[5]A Korambu is a temporary dam constructed across the mouth of channels using materials like brushwood, mud, and grass. The structure is designed to raise the water level in the canal and divert water into field channels, ensuring efficient irrigation.
[6]Land to which local people have a right to farm
[7]Landholder; A superior proprietor who paid land revenue to the government.

would receive immediate benefit from the additional irrigation provided by the Project. He assessed the potential for second crop production as 53,912 acres from the same area. His conclusions that the enterprise would be cost effective were to prove crucial to establishing the viability of the Project.

John Pennycuick studied the agricultural way of life and developed an understanding of the culture of farmers within the canal and tank fed areas of cultivation. He concluded that the motivation of ryot[8] farmers to extract the highest possible yield from the land was a key factor in the success of the Project and expressed every confidence in their achieving the anticipated utilisation of the available water. He also endorsed the conclusion that the network of canals, anicuts and tanks would need to be refurbished as an integral part of the Periyar Project.

When the importance of the Periyar Project to improve the resilience of the long-term agricultural economy was realised by the Madras Engineering Group in 1880, the proposal was put at the top of the priority list of projects for government approval. The feasibility and technical solution for a masonry dam gained official approval from the Madras Engineering Group in 1882, when the, then, Major Pennycuick was authorised to draw up detailed plans. The plans were definitely sanctioned by the Secretary of State for India in 1884 but the Government of India refused the allocation of funding until 1887, when the Project was authorised with urgency.

This delay in authorisation to proceed is difficult to attribute simply to funding and bureaucracy. Ostensibly the delay was

---

[8]Tenant farmers who paid revenue to the Zamindar Landholders.

financial but there was another aspect that could have played a significant part in the delay. It appears that although the Furens Masonry Dam on the River Loire, completed in 1866 was successful, a number of masonry gravity dams constructed around this time on the theoretical principle of a gravity dam defined by J. Augustine DeSazilly had failed.

It is understandable that information about French engineering projects was unavailable at this time, but a more accessible example was available to the Madras Engineering Group, in the construction of the Vrynwy Dam in Wales. Completed in 1888 to provide a water supply to the rapidly growing city of Liverpool, the Vrynwy Dam was the first masonry dam in Britain which was designed as a gravity dam. The design was preceded by a vigorous debate about whether it should be an earthen or a masonry dam. The water committee of the Vrynwy Dam convened a review to properly understand the strength and resilience of the masonry mix and the stability of the gravity design. By 1885 after exhaustive survey experimental testing and review the chairman appointed to the committee Mr Aitken concluded that the material and design of a masonry gravity dam were stronger than had been anticipated and above all secure[9]. Since the Madras Engineering Group could have been reluctant to release permission for the Periyar Project without evidence of the security of design of a masonry dam it is probable that the evidence of the research behind the Vrynwy Dam was needed before permission could be granted for the project to proceed.

---

[9] Supplement to The Engineer dated 15th July 1892

Frequent references in the letters and the engineering report which seemed to support this as a possible reason for delay but the communications and technical transfer of engineering knowledge are not obvious apart from references in the engineering report and in letters. It is clear that Major Pennycuick returned to Britain on at least one occasion to obtain supplies and it would be reasonable to suppose that he consulted about the design and construction of newly invented masonry dams before proceeding with the Periyar Project.

VICTORIAN PLANNING

Preparation and Planning

Detailed planning supported by accurate survey defined the Periyar Project. Many of the drawings and maps are reproduced in the "Periyar Project" by A T Mackenzie. The height of the dam at 155 feet was calculated by the quantity of water and depth of reservoir needed to provide a continuous water supply into the Vaigai River.

Whilst bureaucratic delay was holding up the Periyar Project Major John Pennycuick was planning the component parts of the Project. The crucial dynamic was the continuity of water flow into the watershed cutting and tunnel in sufficient quantity to irrigate the farmland in the Vaigai Valley. He calculated that 6815 million cubic feet of water would need to be available above the sill to the watershed cutting to achieve the assurance of supply. The crest of the escape would therefore have to be set at 144 feet above the river datum, with a sill for the watershed cutting at 113 feet above datum to impound the volume of water required as shown in the following diagram. This meant that the dam would have to be built up to a height of 155 feet requiring a crest width at the dam of 1,300 feet between the valley sides.

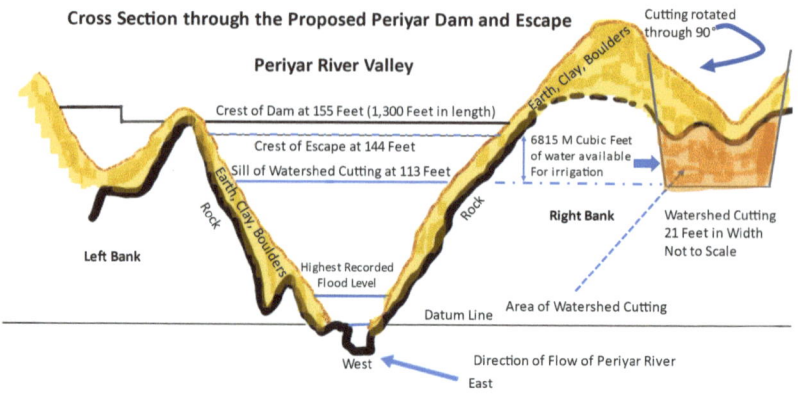

Figure 8. Cross section of the Periyar River showing the proposed dimensions of a Dam

The sill would feed directly into a watershed crossing that would use the profile of a tributary of the Periyar River, The Mulia Panjan which would be modified to establish a fall to the sluice of the tunnel. The tunnel, through granite rock, would have to be drilled concurrently with the development of the dam in order to be ready at the same time as the reservoir filled with water.

The input to the tunnel through a sluice was at a height that required a considerable depth of canal to be dug out using labour. Some of the depth could be achieved by using part of the tributary of the Periyar which could also be dammed to provide a canal and barge transport in the lower 5,000 feet of the cutting. The really deep excavation would need to be carried out in the final 2500 feet of the cutting, running up to the sluice at the tunnel head.

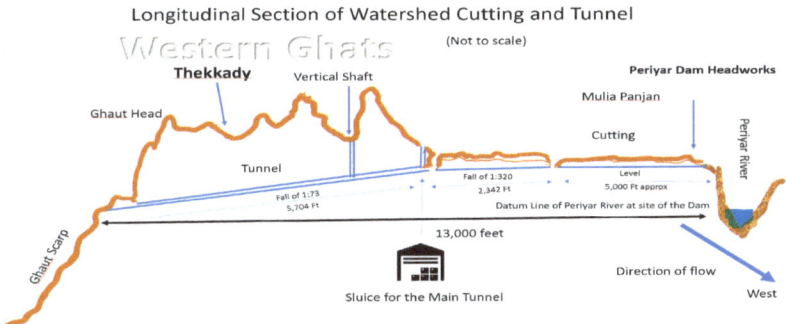

Figure 9. Section of the Watershed showing the Tunnel

The bore, length and fall of the tunnel was specified to syphon and regulate the required flow of water. The survey of the tunnel was conducted and recorded personally by John Pennycuick, who described how he aligned the ends of the tunnel using innovative techniques using an Eckhold Omnimeter to cross seven heavily forested ridges to the site of the input sluice on the Mulia Panjan, a tributary of the Periyar River.

At this stage, the plans were based on occasional reconnaissance along a narrow cart track from the Ghaut Spur Road to a Lower camp as established below the scarp face of the Western Ghats Mountains. This planning engaged Major John Pennycuick until his appointment as Chief Engineer in 1882

The Logistic Challenge

Much of the construction work would take place up to 15 miles from the nearest road at its furthest extent, 3000 feet high in the Western Ghats, in mountains shrouded by dense jungle. These preparations preoccupied John Pennycuick between the time when he was appointed Chief Engineer in 1882 and the implementation of the Project in 1887. Establishing a simple cart track from the road at Lower Camp to the Periyar Dam Headworks was a feat of exploration in itself. John Pennycuick had to apply all the ingenuity he had learned as a junior commander in the Abyssinia Campaign of 1867 to establish reliable transport required for heavy logistic services.

Planning the Supply Lines

Men and materials had to be moved up the 1,500 foot scarp face and navigate round several ridges before building a dam on the Periyar River. A wire ropeway to surmount the Ghaut, as the scarp face was known; a canal system to cross the Western Ghats, and a railway and cutting were all considered to move cement, lime for mortar and surkhi[10] bricks for the face of the Dam from Lower Camp over treacherous landscape to the headworks. With extraordinary foresight, John Pennycuick sourced the hardcore for the construction of the dam from local granite rock and sand from the area of the dam. This meant that the bulk of material could be extracted locally, limiting the heavy lifting of material required from the Vaigai valley plain to cement, lime and surkhi and specialist materials.

---

[10]Surkhi makes cement mortars and concretes more water proof, more resistant to alkalies and to salt solutions than those in which no surkhi is used. Surkhi mixed in cement concrete has been used in some of the big dams and other massive works in India since the Periyar Project. This admixture is known to reduce the temperature rise during hydration in a mass cement concrete and reduce cracking. A technical innovation of the Periyar Project.

Figure 10. Establishing supply lines from Lower Camp to the Periyar Dam Headworks

Manpower

Manpower of up to 6,000 labourers with a variety of specialisms was needed, but these could only be engaged for eight months of the year (referred to as "The Season[11]") because of endemic fevers between March and June. The administrative centres at Thekkady and the dam headworks were established to house and care for the wellbeing of the workforce. Recruiting on this scale at such a remote location in conditions that were known to be dangerous was the responsibility of Mr E R Logan. Initially he drew on labourers from the local village of Cumbum who were farmers by trade and returned to their village at sowing time in October. The search for people with specialisms in masonry, wood working and machine operation extended to towns of Madurai, Cochi,

---

[11]For the Periyar Project, this was generally between July and the following March.

Tinnevelli and beyond, with financial incentives to attract the right disciplines.

Figure 11. Recruiting Local Workers for the Periyar Project

The Interlocking System

By March 1888, the end of the first season of work, an interlocking logistic chain was in place. From Lower Camp a 16,610-foot wire ropeway provided a conveyor belt up the 1,500 foot scarp face for the materials required for constructing the dam.

Beside all the transport was a cart track, initially for labourers to transition from Lower Camp to Thekkady for registration, then to go on foot to the headworks camp. The cart track could only be used for carrying construction materials if bullocks were available which was slow and uncertain especially during rain. This mode of transport was labour intensive and therefore expensive.

There was intense interest in developing more efficient means of transport, including an extension of the wire ropeway, a road, canal and even a railway which was John Pennycuick's preferred means of resource transfer. Each of the options required different routes which would have to navigate the seven ridges and deep, vegetated and waterlogged valleys. He had been impressed by the efficiency, reliability and carrying capacity of the rail service established in hinterland of the Abyssinia Campaign, but this was to prove too costly and circuitous except for the final leg to the dam headworks from a weir.

The chosen approach was to develop a canal network despite the fact that it would only go so far as the sluice for the main tunnel. The watershed cutting, which would be a water conduit, had been marked out and merged with the head of the Mulia Panjan tributary by the time work was due to begin at the dam headworks. A series of 13 locks were designed to bring up the water level for moving supplies down to the headworks but these were replaced by 3 weirs and transhipment arrangements after persistent leaking at the locks.

Driving this network across the Western Ghats ready to begin work at the dam site by July 1888 meant that work had to begin on the tunnel at the head of the Ghaut scarp face at the same time as the dam. The flow of logistics to the dam site was dependent on the component communications working at full efficiency and in synchrony. The wire ropeway could operate to transport 4 tonnes of material per hour for 8 hours per day. The material had to be taken away from the hill crest initially by bullock cart but later by canal at least from the sluice gate towards the dam site. The canal locks however failed to work and the weirs that replaced them used transshipment techniques which were cumbersome and frequently disrupted by heavy rain.

The Final Plans Vision

The connectedness of the communication system by early 1888 enabled the Governor of Madras, Lord Connemara, accompanied by the Secretary to the Government, Colonel Hasted RE, to visit the proposed site of the dam. Undoubtedly John Pennycuick, by then promoted Colonel, would have unrolled a plan of the proposed dam for the Governor to inspect and to explain the approach for damming the river as part of his brief. The plan recorded in the Periyar Project, showed John Pennycuick's intent for construction of the dam in detail.

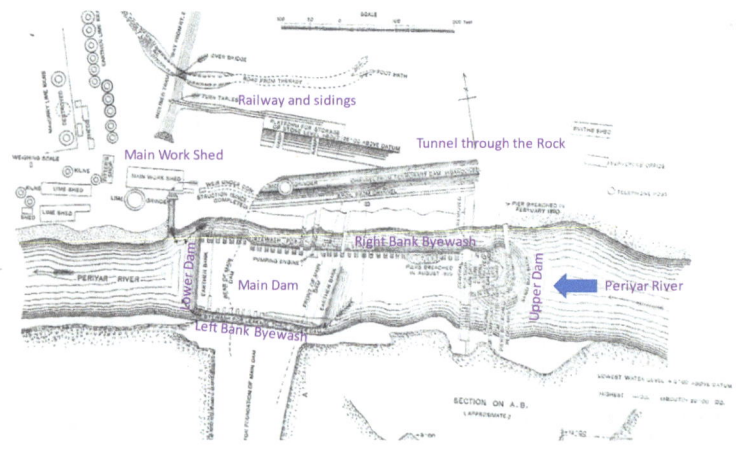

Figure 12. Diagram of the proposed Layout of the Periyar Dam

The plan contains aspects of the development that record later events such as breaches in the byewash that occurred in the following year, added retrospectively on the diagram but it also contains elements that were not fully implemented such as the tunnel parallel to the right bank byewash.

The ambitious plan for development of the main dam was conceived to allow construction using granite rock from the south or left bank to be drawn down onto the path of the Periyar River for masonry fill. An upper dam would be constructed to absorb the energy of the river by sending water down the main right bank byewash and also a less voluminous left bank byewash would provide additional diversion.

The right bank byewash would be defined by a line of piers that could be shuttered leaving a water free space in front of the main dam for construction of foundations and the first stage of the main dam. The piers would lead water to a turbine enclosed by the main workshop which would produce power for breaking rocks and mixing water and lime. A lower dam would be constructed to create working space behind the main dam for construction.

The plan includes a tunnel seen above the right bank byewash through the rock to take excess water. Colonel John Pennycuick was resolutely opposed to this approach since it was vulnerable to blockage from the debris running in the river. This would risk overwhelming construction works and destroy any progress. His departure from the proposed plan would create a significant rift with the Madras Engineering Group. Perhaps this diagram which included the tunnel began a long-lasting dispute about how the excess water from surges or freshers should be absorbed.

The tunnel was never built but Colonel John Pennycuick innovated with other techniques that would ensure the survival of the dam. The alternative approaches that he implemented were regarded as unprofessional and insubordinate that would risk removal from his appointment. One significant advantage of the remoteness of the site was to give him the opportunity make decisions without the headquarters breathing down his neck and he took full advantage of that situation to innovate without contradiction whilst building the dam.

ENGAGEMENT WITH THE PERIYAR RIVER

The development of the Periyar Dam was scheduled to take five seasons. Having established the supply lines in the first season, and demonstrated the plan to the Governor of Madras, the main effort during the second season would be constructing the foundation for the main dam spanning the river between July 1888 and April 1889.

The Tiger in the Periyar

The drop of 3,000 feet from the upper reaches of the catchment of the Periyar River gave great power to surges in the flow of the river created by storms that were beyond the horizon. These surges, amplified after the junction with the Mullayar River, seven miles upstream from the dam site, could arrive very suddenly and violently at the site of the dam. The river could rise, and the volume of water increase to between four and six times in the space of three hours. Like a tiger attack, the surges would be sudden, unexpected and quite overwhelming. This unpredictability had held up work during the second season.

Second Season Shock

Confidence in the plan was shaken when a deep chasm was discovered in the riverbed sometime during mid 1888 just as people and resources were being assembled for the second season effort. The void was estimated at 80 feet wide x 20 feet deep running at least from the proposed upper dam to below the site. This chasm, masked by the fast-flowing river, had to be filled before work could commence on the foundation of the main dam. The chasm not only presented a considerable water void to fill with available rock, but also acted as a natural focus for the energy of the river magnifying its destructive power. This effect would be at its greatest during the monsoon periods when the river was flowing fastest, generally between March and July, then later in the year between November and January. Despite several pathetic attempts at dropping rock into the chasm an unusually rainy season prevented the engineers from filling the chasm.

It became clear that the Periyar Project would have to be abandoned if a solution could not be found during the second working season and before the southwest monsoon in 1889 when the high flow rate of the river would prevent any further attempt to fill the chasm. In the absence of John Pennycuick who was visiting Britain to procure logistic supplies, several options were considered by the officers on site which would require significant changes to the plans including moving the site of the dam further upstream where the chasm was less pronounced. The situation offered no easy options to the operations team and decisions were at an *impasse* which gave the entire operation a great sense of despondency. Efforts to bridge the chasm continued from piers constructed into the river from both banks but sandbags and rocks were carried away "like pieces of paper".

Breaking the impasse of the Chasm

On his return, John Pennycuick, was faced with the dilemma of bridging the chasm or of relocating the site of the main dam at considerable cost. The latter would undoubtedly require authorisation from the headquarters, time for reconnaissance and extensive replanning.

In a course of action that was developed from careful observation of the river during flooding episodes, John Pennycuick established a candidate solution using pre-fabricated wooden trestles built to match the profile of the chasm. This was undoubtedly the last chance to bridge the chasm before the end of the second season and the monsoon. In a risky manoeuvre, the preconstructed trestles were dropped into the chasm from barges, then reinforced with sandbags, to act as a bulwark to the main dam foundation from March 1889. These provided a sufficiently watertight solution for the masonry labourers to lay the foundation of the main dam before the presumed burst of the southwest monsoon in June 1889. The following diagram shows the location of the trestles in relation to the upper dam, and to the area of the main dam where they were to form the underpinning for the foundations.

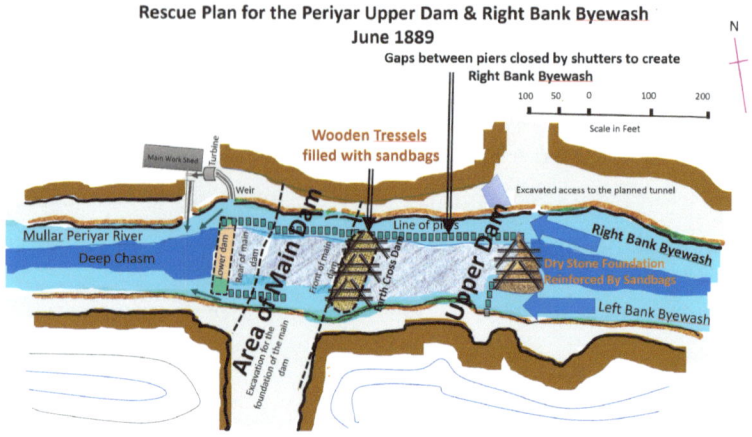

Figure 13. Establishment of secure foundations by the deployment of wooden trestles

At the same time, a byewash was established along the right bank of the river, marked by a line of piers, to channel the normal flow of the river estimated at $1,600^3$ feet per second and drive a turbine for powering machinery in the main workshop. An additional byewash on the left bank was designed to take water away from enclosures formed once the upper dam had been constructed.

Thus the architecture for the foundation of the dam had been established just in time for the third season which would secure the site of the main dam and enable construction to continue. The existence of a chasm in the river may have prevented the development of a dam and the scale of the geological anomaly could yet undermine the construction. But the resourcefulness of John Pennycuick and his innovative approach created an original solution that would provide the best chance of success for the Periyar Project.

Figure 14. Early photograph of the Periyar Dam showing foundation Outline (flow from the left)

The Third Season

The river was in spate from the start of the third season in July 1889. A brief respite in November allowed an upper dam to be constructed to protect the working space in front of the area for the main dam. This allowed the space to be pumped dry ready to construct the front wall.

The earliest photograph of the dam site taken from an elevation on the right or northern bank shows the upper and lower dams with people working in the area in between which appears to be pumped dry. The area of the left bank adjacent to the dry area has clearly been exploited for materials used in the construction of the dams. The photograph, taken later in 1889, is evidence of the success of the bridging of the chasm and the establishment of foundations for the construction of the main dam.

Two successive surges recorded on the 17th and 28th December demolished the upper dam, byewash piers and much of the pumping apparatus. The working area in front of the coffer dam was inundated without any prospect of recovery after the damage inflicted. Again, there was the prospect of having to abandon the construction of the dam before the onset of the next monsoon season.

Once more, John Pennycuick demonstrated engineering ingenuity. A cross-dam earthen wall was constructed tight up against the foundation of the main dam with enough clearance to drain the foot of the front wall and build up the front face of the dam. This allowed the main dam to be extended across the river with sufficient height, assessed as 25 feet, to avoid submergence and destruction during surges. This was set by John Pennycuick as the target for the season but the large volumes of materials that had to be processed to fill the distance between the front and rear walls was proving demanding for the manufacturing process of masonry.

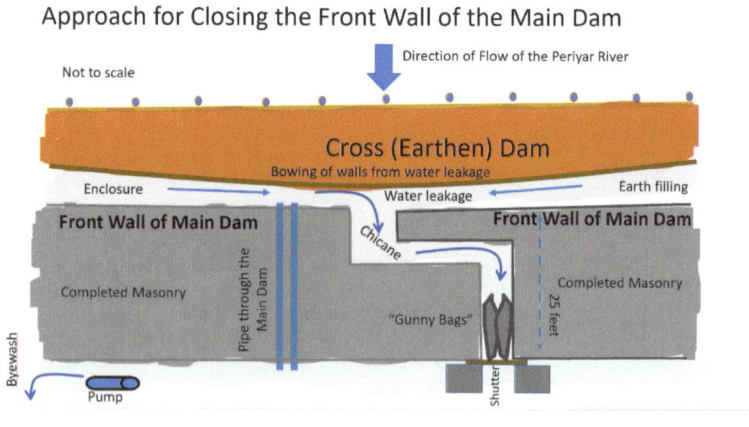

Figure 15. **Closing the Front Wall of the Main Dam**

The window of opportunity for getting the main dam front wall elevated to be secure was so brief that compromises had to be made in the plan. First, to separate construction of the front and back walls. This was to enable sufficient effort to be committed to get the height of the front wall up before the next surge which could destroy the new structure. Labourers worked night and day in teams to staunch the flow of water so that new masonry could be used to construct the wall. John Pennycuick described this period as "The most anxious, difficult and exhausting of any that had come within his experience" in his report to government. He and his staff received the thanks of the government.

The following diagram shows the cross-section profile of the front and rear of the main dam with the cross dam protecting the front of the main dam.

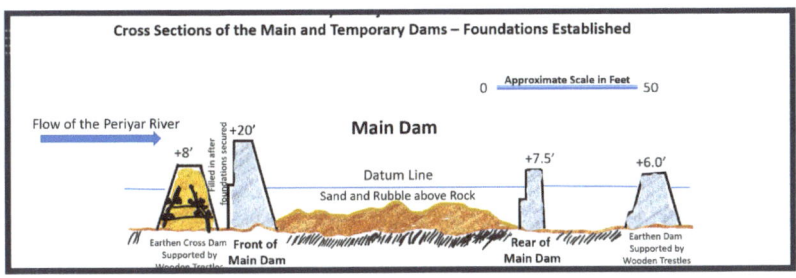

Figure 16. Diagram of the Front and Rear of the Main Dam

By mid-April 1890, the front wall stood at 20 feet, still 5 feet short of the target (with the exception of a lower sill on the left bank side). The leakage into the main dam enclosure resulting from the separation of front and back walls was undermining the nascent structure which further surges might easily overwhelm.

A massive surge soon arrived. A storm surge on the 19th April 1890 overtopped the front wall and carried tons of mud and debris into the Main Dam enclosure. The newly constructed wall held firm, however, allowing the upward development of the Main Dam as soon as conditions permitted. Meanwhile the submergence of the Dam persisted into July as shown in the photograph below:

Figure 17. Periyar River in flood over Main Dam Foundations

Keeping the Tiger at bay

Until this flood, the byewash had successfully syphoned away excess flow except when it overtopped the front wall. With the experience of the previous two seasons culminating with the latest surge, John Pennycuick realised that the surges could exceed ten times the regular flow, and exceptionally reach 120,00³ feet per second or 100 times the regular flow. This volume of water would raise the river level by 35 feet, for which there was clear flood line evidence, and would certainly exceed the capacity of a closed syphon, endangering the structure of the dam.

This evidence was to become reality when, in January 1891, the engineering team at the main dam was beset by a surprise "fresh". The officer Taylor wrote to Colonel John Pennycuick dated 23rd January /91:

My dear Colonel

We had a big fresh here on the night of the 20th. I'm writing officially about it but you would like to know sooner than that will reach you. The river had been at about 17 and 18 feet for a day or two before on the 20th at 10:00 PM it was 17.8 on the upper gauge. At about 1130 the wall was topped and it reached its highest at about 1:00 AM which was 28.19 or three feet over the wall. It rose so suddenly that it cut off Mackenzie Logan and Rosario who were at the engine brackets on the dam wall. They could not get up on the wall as the water was rushing down on them from 28 feet and they could not get along the wall to the bridge as the water was washing over them too. All they could do was to get on the boiler of the engine and trust to luck not to be washed away. There they were for 4-5 mortal hours with the water rushing through the wrecks and logs every now and then jamming adjacent to the engine which of course was shaking a good deal and literally expecting every moment to be their last as no one could have lived in the rush below. When a log dashed against the engine and made it shake, they were in an awful position and for such a time too they were of course drenched through and bitterly cold. Fortunately, except Mackenzie has a bad cold, they were none the worse for wear. That old engine has added another big leaf to its Laurel crown and deserves more than ever the to be embalmed. If it had given way there was no chance for them. The wall stood it splendidly not a stone being displaced.

This letter was complemented by an addendum by A T Mackenzie who wrote:

> Yesterday at 10:00 PM the river was at 17.80 and I went to bed at 11:00 PM without anxiety. At 11:15 PM it was over the gauge (+ 22), at 11:35 PM it was over the front wall and I had to wade to get to the barges and engine on the other side of the dam which had to be tied up. I was there only 10 minutes and could only just wade back to the 12 horsepower engine where Ernest Logan and Rosario were trying to let off steam from the boiler. When we had settled this the water was over the side wall and we could not get to the bridge nor could we get back along the front wall as it rose still we had to climb on the engine which stood bravely but was far from dry as a lodgement.

> The water rose to plus 28 in front and about plus 15 or so in the rear and I expected the engine to slide or the front wall to go any moment. At about 2:00 AM it (water level) began to fall and was down to + 26 at 5:30 AM when they got a rope from the bridge to the engine and we hauled ourselves through the water to the bridge. There was a sad want of resource about them all. We thought of a lot of ways of

getting a rope or a boat but no one else did. Perhaps our wits were sharpened?

I have been all over the dam this morning (+ 22 above and + 6 below) and there was hardly a stone displaced I wanted to begin by pumping but everyone was asleep. Of course there is a good deal of loss of small things planks flumes steam piping etc but nothing serious the upper bridge of the two of course has gone.

Taylor will doubtless give you a detailed account I thought I would just let you know as I was writing by this post but just now I want to go to sleep badly your Earnest (Logan) is a brick

your sincerely A T Mackenzie

The newly constructed front wall of the main dam was now like a target for the elemental forces whose capricious nature could easily overwhelm and destroy the dam as demonstrated by the account by the officers Taylor and Mackenzie above.

The geological evidence was clear from the experience of the engineering team that showed there was imminent danger from being overwhelmed by flooding of another order of magnitude. Another way of controlling the flow of water over the dam had to be found.

Dual System of Vents and Byewash

The Government's recommendation for closed syphons through the dam was vehemently opposed by John Pennycuick. Closed syphons, with a fixed volume, he argued, would undoubtedly be overwhelmed by the quantity of water in surges and would be liable to catastrophic blockage from trees and vegetation.

Instead, John Pennycuick implemented a dual system of vents, at the same time upscaling the byewash as the height of the dam increased. This approach was adopted during the fourth season from June 1890 to April 1891 when the front wall height reached 25 feet, and was still vulnerable to over topping from the most serious surges.

The original right bank byewash was upscaled by shuttering off the line of piers and diverting the flow of the river progressively higher up the bank of the river as shown in principle in the following diagram.

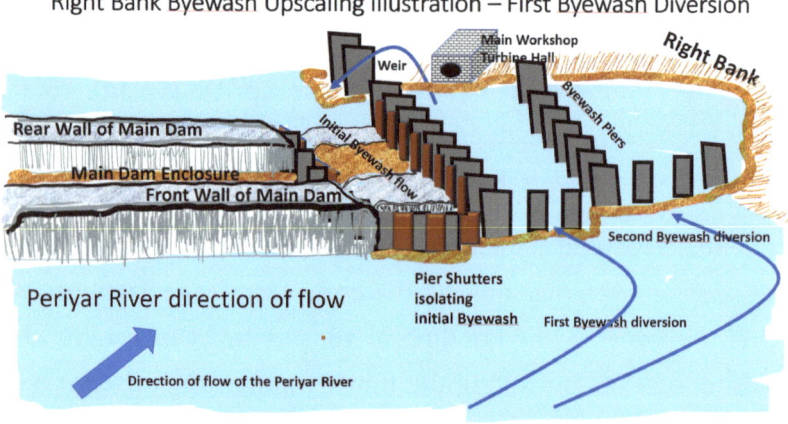

Figure 18. Right Bank Byewash Upscaling - first Byewash Diversion

A photograph taken in October 1890 clearly shows the line of byewash piers running down the right bank of the river between the main dam front wall and the main dam rear wall but continuing on below the rear wall towards the site of the workshops. This photograph was perhaps taken before introduction of vents into the main dam front wall but it is likely that the photographer would not have been allowed to photograph the vent because they were not permitted by the Madras Engineering Group headquarters.

Figure 19. Periyar Dam showing byewash upscaling to second line of piers

Secure construction of the main dam depended on the efficiency of vents passing water through the dam in addition to the byewash without endangering the structure. Whilst these worked satisfactorily, they hindered the uniform upward development of the front wall.

The following diagram is an example of how the vents would have been developed with an active vent and a vent in development. The active vent would have been developed first with the vent in development starting at a higher level. When the main dam front wall was elevated the active vent would be closed by lowering a caisson in front of the vent supported by a concrete shelf. A nearly watertight seal would be established between the caisson and the wall to allow labourers to fill in the vent whilst work continues on the wall. Meanwhile the vent in development would be prepared ready to drain the raised river level during a surge. Thus the capability to drain the water from surges would keep pace with the upward development of the main dam front wall.

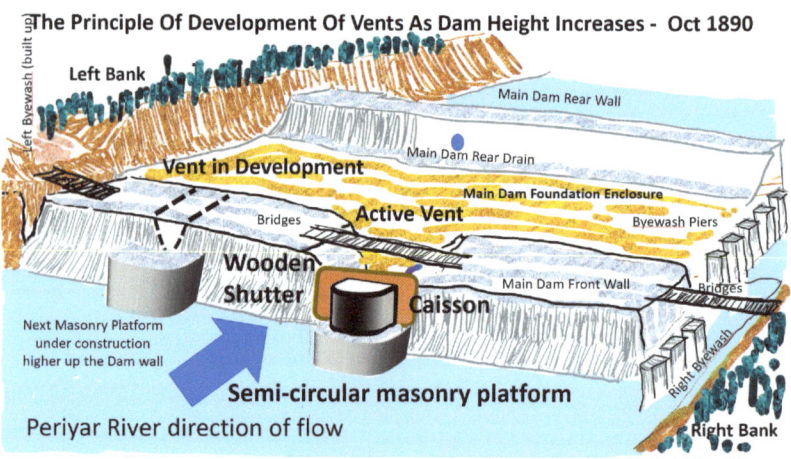

Figure 20. Temporary Vent development as dam height increases

Construction of the main dam was slowed at this critical time by interruption to supplies because a weir on the Muliar Panjan was breached by fallen trees in January 1891, just as upward development on the main dam was gathering pace. A surge in the river drove water up the Muliar Panjan tributary and felled trees which blocked the canal. This meant that barges could not use the canal for transport of heavy materials and the following photograph shows the impact of fallen trees on weir 3 on the Muliar Panjan where heavy material would be transferred to the rail sidings for delivery to the dam.

Figure 21. Weir number 3 breached interrupting supplies

With slow progress on the elevation of the front wall of the main dam because of interruption to supply lines the works were particularly vulnerable. During the fourth working season, the system of vents and byewash successfully kept the works secure and progress was made to achieve the 25 feet elevation of the main dam front wall before the end of the season in March 1891.

Taming the Tiger in the Fifth Season

From June 1891, the beginning of the fifth season, the pace of construction quickened until October. The supply of materials had to be delivered by ox cart as the canal system deteriorated with landslips and damage making the canal system all but impossible. With good organisation, however, progress was made on the next important stage of construction which was to infill the main dam enclosure that would bring the front and rear walls of the dam together and improve the security of the structure.

Suddenly, the river levels rose dramatically and submerged the main dam on five separate occasions in November and December 1891 as if to confound ambitions for filling the enclosure. The ferocity of the river destroyed 20,000 cubic feet of concrete and 7,000 cubic feet of rubble and masonry. In a potentially more destructive development, boulders of ¾ ton were rolled along the riverbed to threaten the main dam front wall.

The repair of the main dam and development effort following the series of inundations required a large amount of additional manpower. The work had to be carried out by hand and the workmen had to clamber from the bank onto the dam with makeshift bridges, then to cross the vents to deposit cement and mortar on the main dam enclosure.

Despite this dreadful setback, the work rate increased and by March 1892 the main dam front wall had reached 37' with the reservoir offering a significant buffer to surges from the raging river. Progress on the construction and upward development is shown in the following photograph where the main front wall with temporary vent is shown with the elevated area between the main dam front wall and the rear with considerable debris swept to the rear of the main dam enclosure by the floods.

Figure 22. Main Dam Front Wall Elevated towards 37'

However, as if to confound progress, a further monumental surge in April 1892 when the river rose 20 feet carried away two piers in the turbine weir and overturned the bridge used for access to the main dam enclosure. The main dam, with a substantial rear wall at 23 feet and the enclosure level at 13 feet above datum, was now a secure structure which could withstand overtopping by the river. More significantly for the further development of the main dam, the absorbing capacity of the reservoir acted as a buffer against fluctuations in the depth of the river. The tiger had been successfully tamed.

Dash for Destination in the Sixth Season

Although the damn was now secure from damaging floods, the possibility of reaching the height of 155 feet as the destination for the main dam from the existing 37 feet seemed unlikely without significant change of tempo.

During the sixth season from June 1892, the byewash was augmented a second time, but a permanent vent was designed in anticipation of the dam front wall reaching 60 feet. In John Pennycuick's own words "A vent of more permanent description through which water could be discharged until work was completed". The significance of this apparent concession to a closed syphon was that the tempo of construction work could be increased along the top of the main dam, bringing together the front and back walls as the enclosure was filled above the height of 60 feet.

In the meantime, work on construction of the main dam intensified with over 4,000 labourers deployed to the headworks from June 1892, filling in the five remaining temporary vents and raising the main dam at a rapid rate. At times, this was fraught with difficulty whilst surges threatened the lower vents. The following photograph shows labourers filling in the largest 25 foot temporary vent during March 1893 which was threatened with being overwhelmed shortly after this photograph was taken.

Figure 23. Filling in Temporary Vents

Meanwhile, the surges of the previous season affected the canal network which had been transporting heavy material from the junction with the wire ropeway near Thekkady. In July 1892, the No 3 Weir, which had been breached the previous season, had transhipment facilities overturned by storms and flooding. Several barges were sunk, denying heavy lift capability for 5 miles of the journey. Repairs were completed by October, but almost immediately, the bund on which the weir was built collapsed. Limestone and surkhi had to be transported by ox cart from the No2 Weir for the remainder of the project.

Figure 24. Number 2 Weir becomes the point from which material sent to the Main Dam

In spite of logistics challenges, upwards progress with construction of the main dam reached 60 feet by March 1893 towards the end of the sixth season. This was the level at which the permanent sluice could be operating through the width of the main dam. By this point in the construction the front and rear walls were at a similar height with only a small depression in the enclosure.

A Permanent Vent for Victory

It seems that John Pennycuick authorised implementation of the permanent vent without reference to government. He had reached an *impasse* with the authorities over drainage of the river and chose to proceed with his own design at great risk to his career.

Somehow the government of India heard about the structure and held the Madras Government to account. John Pennycuick was forced to account for his actions. His cogent argument highlighted that the dam had reached sufficient height to absorb the energy of the river to justify a permanent vent which could control the level of the reservoir that had been created by the dam. His design showed that the level of the reservoir could now be safely controlled by use of his design of permanent vent. The permanent vent is shown in the following diagram.

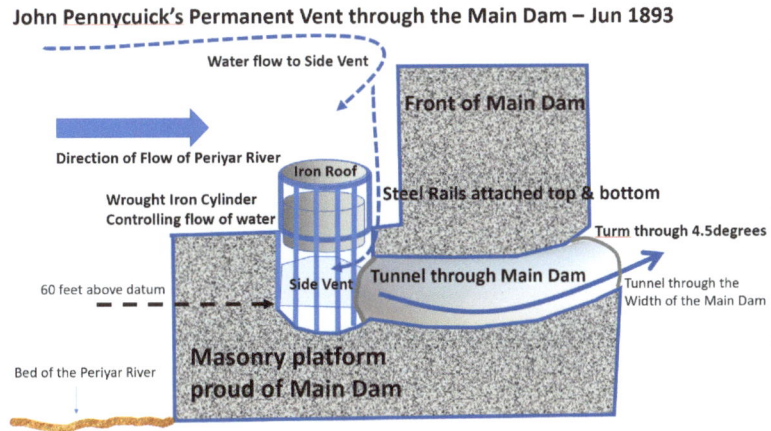

Figure 25. Permanent Vent Design

John Pennycuick's single-minded and determined defence of his design saw off any further interference before the completion of the dam.

Epidemic In the Seventh Season

A more sinister threat to the construction manpower become apparent during 1892 as steadily rising numbers of the workforce were reporting sick outside the fever season. This was the first year in which records were being properly recorded and the data shows a decline in those reporting sick after the fever season between March and July. From the beginning of the seventh season in July 1893 the proportion of the workforce reporting sick began at the high level of 40% and after an initial dip, increased at both the headworks and Thekkady to 60%.

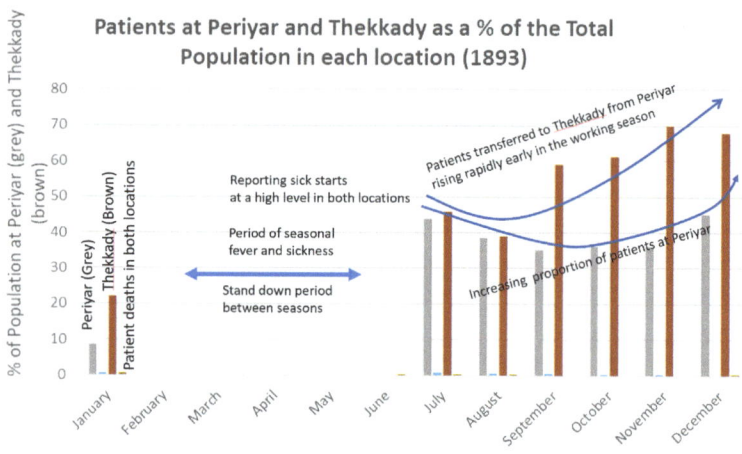

Monthly % of an average population of 3191 (Periyar) and 1051 (Thekkady)
Recorded deaths overall - 83

Figure 26. Increasing Proportion of workers reporting sick

This tragedy struck just as manpower was crucially needed to complete the construction of the dam. In the following year of 1894 the numbers reporting sick and a death toll of 138 forced the administration to close and burn the camps at the headworks and treat the earth with quicklime. It was generally accepted that the groundwater had become contaminated resulting in a cholera epidemic. Consequently, the labourers' camp was moved to the south bank of the river before work could continue in the following, eighth season.

A Convenient Respite from Surges and Disease

With the height of the main dam at 80 feet by the beginning of the eighth season, and a refreshed labour force following the outbreak of cholera, an unprecedented drought allowed the completion of the dam without surges.

The water level of the reservoir was allowed to rise to 60 feet in September 1894 and water flowed through the permanent vent successfully. The importance of this was that construction of the main dam could accelerate unhindered by the need for temporary vents. The following photograph shows the main dam at about 60 feet with permanent vent under construction. The wall would increase to over 80 feet before the operation of the permanent vent could be trialled in September which took place without incident.

Figure 27. Main Dam front and back wall development accelerating

Tunnelling through the Western Ghats

Meanwhile, the prospect of good progress with the main dam gave added impetus to the drilling of the tunnel through the watershed of the Western Ghats. The main effort was applied to the north-going tunnel from a central shaft which met with the Madurai Tunnel with astonishing accuracy in October 1894. All that remained was to link up with the tunnel from the sluice gates which was quickly achieved to provide a continuous tunnel 12 feet wide and 7.5 feet high. The sluice draining from the watershed cutting was a sophisticated mechanism that would regulate the water between 1,600 and 2,166³ feet per second.

Figure 28. Sluice Gates into the Tunnel

Despite the slow progress of construction of the tunnel due to the density of the granite rock, the completion synchronised with development of the main dam. The watershed cutting was near to completion.

Figure 29. Watershed Cutting

Flanking Dams

The Right Bank Spillway was developed using a geological spur from the area of the headworks to provide an overflow beyond the Right Bank in case the main dam was in danger of overtopping. This was an innovative expedient designed during the planning but envisaged as a contingency. The Spillway became vital during the recent signal flooding events during 2018 and 2021 to release water downstream in a controlled manner to prevent destruction of 19 dams on the Periyar River further downstream. Construction of the Baby Dam became problematic during the final year of construction because the geomorphology prevented the extension of the main dam using masonry up to the ridge forming the far edge of the system. Instead, the Baby Dam had to be constructed as part earthen dam and so could not be used as an additional spillway.

The following photograph shows the Baby Dam, main dam and the right bank spillway

Figure 30. Main and flanking Dams development from upstream

The Grand Opening

Such was the pace of construction that the main dam was raised to 115 feet by the end of March 1895 and the water in the reservoir was allowed to rise to the sill of the watershed cutting, thus testing the ability of the tunnel to accept a flow of water and send it to the plains of the Vaigai Valley and the canal network around Madura. The volume and rate of flow of water from the reservoir was exactly as John Pennycuick had specified.

His Excellency Lord Wenlock formally declared the Dam operational at the site of the sluice of the tunnel in October 1895 in a ceremony attended by, amongst other dignitaries, the Bishop of Travancore. The significance of this attendance was that Periyar Dam lay within the State of Travancore (now lying within Kerala) and the land leased on a long to the State of Madura (now Tamil Nadu).

Colonel John Pennycuick was made Companion of the Star of India (C.S.I.) in 1895.

Figure 31. Opening Ceremony of the Periyar Project

Figure 32. Lord Wenlock and Project Staff

Reporting Completion of Construction

The opening was promptly reported by the Royal Geographical Society in the Monthly Record of November 1895 in the following terms:

"The project discussed at various times from 1808 onwards, but only put into execution in 1885 upon plans prepared by Colonel Pennycuick for diverting the upper course of the Periyar from its normal direction towards the west coast, and carrying it across the watershed to the opposite side of the peninsula, has lately been completed……

Its object is to draw upon the superabundant water-supply of the western slope derived from the moisture-laden south-west monsoon, for the benefit of the area to the east, which is always exposed to the risk of famine, owing to its small and precarious rainfall."

BAPTISM FROM THE GHATS

Irrigation Infrastructure

A comprehensive modernisation programme of the irrigation infrastructure had been undertaken as a major part of the Periyar Project to improve the control of the water distribution, the capacity and the reliability of the supply. To quote the report, "*In the course of the work, the whole of the canals were realigned, and every masonry work was designed afresh* ". The development of the reaches from the rivers and the branches from the canals made the additional water supply available to a wide area of the Vaigai River catchment area.

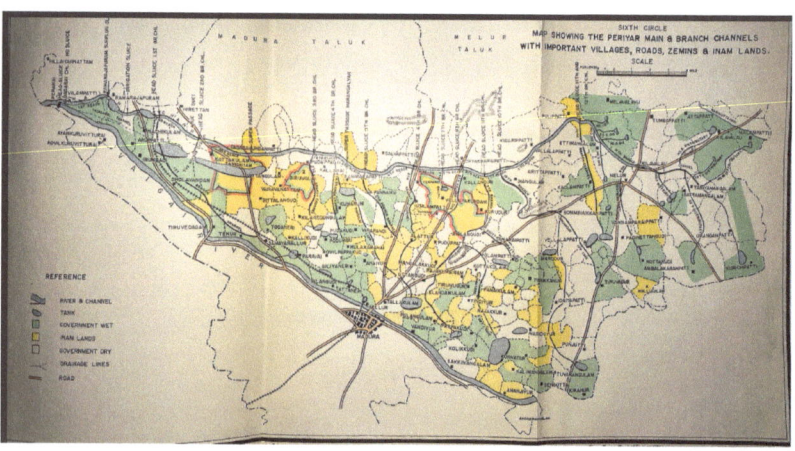

Figure 33. Network of canals for irrigation from "the Periyar Project"

The water from the Periyar Project was available through a network of canals, dams (anicuts) and water storage tanks from the rivers Vairavanar and Suruliyar which flow into the Vaigai. From the tunnel to the junction of the Suruliyar with the Vaigai at Theni is about 46 miles. From there to the bend south eastwards a major anicut on the Vaigai River, is about 40 miles. Thereafter, the Periyar water Main Canal is 38 miles to Thirupuvanam but supports a complex network with 12 branches to the north and northeast of Madurai. The Main Canal is 6 feet deep with a bottom width of 100 feet at the head with a capacity to deliver 2016^3 feet a second. This must have seemed like a miracle to the farmers. The water storage tanks were reinforced by the Madras Engineer Group revetting the canal structure and rinsing the sand that had accumulated as Florence Nightingale had recommended, thus capitalising on the traditional facilities that were vital for local water supply.

The scale of the irrigation network can be appreciated from the component parts detailed by Nelson in his Madura Manual of 1868. According to Nelson in the rotwary areas of Madura there were 5688 tanks of which many were fed by 588 river channels, 27 spring channels and 376 anicuts, and irrigated an area of 182,887 acres. At the time of Nelson's writing the Vaigai river was about 250 kilometres long but had only four masonry anicuts of which two are of no use. Of the functioning anicuts the first one, the Peranai, was essentially to head up the river to create a gravity flow into the channel. This channel named as Vadakarai on the north bank joins the river after filling a few tanks. The second anicut, Thenkarai on the south bank was to transfer water to the tanks in the adjoining Gundar river basin. All other channels were temporary and seasonal. The 376 anicuts were on the smaller streams and riverlets that were used to divert water into the tanks. These 5688 tanks were in three different river basins - Vaigai, Gundar and Sarugani. However the Vaigai River remained an important source to support them all.

Intended Impact of Periyar Water

The Financial Director of the Madras Engineering Group, Mr Clougstoun, had assumed in 1876 that the water from the Periyar Project would be available to the entire network of rivers, canals, and water tanks lying mostly in the Theni, Dindigul (southern part) and Madurai Taluks. He estimated that the potential cultivable area was approximately 150,000 acres. Much of the area was arable, and amenable to irrigation.

The projection come under scrutiny from the Public Works Minister, Sir Charles Elliot, in 1890, much later during the project. The projection was revised to reclassify the wet and dry land and to incorporate a more accurate assessment of the land likely to yield a second crop. This resulted in a considerable augmentation of the amount of land that could be utilised for a second crop, as John Pennycuick had anticipated, and a consequential increase in the potential revenue. The resulting, revised projections now stretched forward 20 years with net revenue, after charges and interest were deducted, being positive after ten years and increasing in line with the extent of the area to 150,000 acres under irrigation. At its greatest extent in the 21st Century, Periyar Water reached 340,000 acres.

The Consequences of the Periyar Project

How did this Project work in practice? During the first year of settled irrigation from the Periyar Project of 1896 to 1897, 50,106 acres of ryot farmers' occupied wet land and 7,203 acres of second crop were irrigated. This exceeded projections five-fold for first crop, and was about in line with expectation for the second crop. The report commented that there was no reason whatever to believe that the expansion to the expected area would not be normal and uniform.

Furthermore, of the inam and zamindari farm lands 1,217 acres of new first crop and 5225 acres of new second crop were irrigated. Since these landlords represented the leadership in the countryside for the development of cultivable lands, the take-up of irrigation, particularly for second crop represented a significant trend. This leadership was vital to the agricultural revolution that the Periyar Project brought about.

AGRICULTURAL AWAKENING

Technical Hitches

There were two factors affecting delivery in the first year. Firstly, the sluices at the head of the tunnel jammed, which made it impossible to hold back water for the driest part of the year in March, April and May, the very time when the water was most needed. Although this incident had an impact on the farmers' expectations, it was regarded as an insignificant issue technically and the offending sluice was replaced by a more reliable "Stoney's patent shutter" within a short period.

Although this gear failure was regarded as a teething problem, it brought about a major revision of the irrigation infrastructure strategy which should not be underestimated. The rain-fed tanks, which were regarded as redundant with the advent of the water from the Periyar River, were now regarded as useful contingency during the dry months. The rain-fed tanks numbering at least 1,000 in the Madura and Melur taluks would therefore continue to be maintained by the Madras Government.

Vested Interests

The bountiful supply of water caused cultural problems of water utilisation. By the terms of their tenure, the inam and zamindari landlords saw no direct benefit from the spread of irrigation to the ryot farmers and refused to support any extension to irrigation unless they realised some benefit. In some cases, they refused to use the water or allow channels to pass through their land. Inam and zamindari farmers proposed to prohibit ryot farmers' access to irrigation unless they were permitted to draw water without payment. This challenge to vested interests amongst the inam and zamindari landlords, appeared to be voiced by only a minority, whilst the vast majority embraced the availability of water supplies. For those who held out for personal advantage in the form of free access to the water or a lower rate for access to the water, other incentives were offered such as improved banking of the waterways and improved access to tanks. This seemed to resolve the tension over the distribution of water supplies but gave rise to the Irrigation Act which brought into law right of access to publicly owned irrigation for the community.

Cultural Change

The more significant change for the ryot farmers was the sowing and harvesting schedule. The custom had been to sow the first crop in October for the northeast monsoon and reap it in January. A much smaller and more hazardous second crop would then be sown in February to be reaped in April. The Periyar water, as it came to be known, would also be available in June when climatic conditions were right for planting. This would allow much earlier planting and the opportunity for a more reliable second crop.

This required a rescheduling of the ryot farmers' annual planting, growing and harvesting cycle to take full advantage of the availability of water. The practices of the farmers took some time to modify but, in time, and with re-education which came from the Madras Government, the farmers adapted their annual schedule. It must also have required some level of confidence in the community to commit to such a radical alteration to the way of life.

Agricultural Revolution

The great challenge for the future was to extend irrigation to land that was hitherto dry, thus bringing new land under cultivation. Whilst there was potential for this, investment in preparation and fertiliser was necessary to make the land as productive as that already tilled. Locally sourced fertiliser is unavailable from either leaf fall or animal manure, so fertiliser would have to be imported. This investment was beyond the means of local farmers because of poverty.

This situation established the practice of the Government providing agricultural loans whilst, at the same time, importing fertiliser for the ryot farmers. In addition, the Government offered a reduction of 50% in water rate for the first three years of a farmer's conversion of land from dry to wet land, followed by a 25% reduction in the subsequent three years as an incentive to extend land use to hitherto dry lands.

In addition, the Government offered the incentive of digging new irrigation channels free of charge if they were watering in excess of 50 acres. These proved more difficult than envisaged because they had to cross inferior rocky or gravelly land to reach the proximity of ryot farmers. This incentive was adopted in the year 1896/7 for 1,217 acres of new first crop and 5,225 acres of second crop and Mackenzie believed their rate of expansion would continue into the future. Thus, was brought about the change to a market led economy from subsistence farming.

MODEL FOR CLIMATE EMERGENCY

Green Revolution

The analysis of the benefits of Periyar water stopped with irrigation, but John Pennycuick had shown foresight in convening a committee to consider using the fall of water in the upper reaches of the Vaigai river to generate power even before the dam had been completed in 1893. This application of the water was seen to have benefit for manufacturing carbides of calcium and aluminium, powering transport (particularly railways), cotton mills and electric lighting. This proposal was put out to tender in 1897 by the Madras Government, but there was no immediate response. The application of the water for generation of power from 1959 was to become a key requirement in the future of light engineering stimulated by John Pennycuick's initiative and foresight.

The Periyar Project today

The Periyar Dam has been in continuous use for almost 130 years, delivering the designed quantity of water to the Vaigai Valley throughout the year and generating hydroelectric power since 1959. The dam and reservoir have provided additional important functions in recent years, notably flood control of the Periyar River resulting from climate change with signal flood events in 2018 and 2021. The area is now one of the 18 biodiversity protected hotspots of India, a home for endangered species.

A UN Report[12] on the Periyar Dam, which pointed out that the dam had a projected lifespan of 50 years, reported that the structure showed significant flaws and might be at risk of failure. The dam is located in a seismically active area and minor earthquake caused cracks in the dam in 1979 (Rao, 2018), and in 2011 more cracks appeared but it remains sound.

Currently, the decision of how to manage the ageing Periyar dam is hotly debated between the State of Kerala, in which the dam is situated, and Tamil Nadu, which benefits from the water supply, and division of responsibility is working through the Indian court system. A dam failure would be catastrophic: nearly 3.5 million people will be affected (Chowdhury, 2013).

Opportunities for the future

The leadership and vision of John Pennycuick demonstrates the importance of strategic thinking for realising the potential of the Periyar Project. It would be facile to consider solutions without taking account of a context which includes a natural environment which is changing in a volatile and extreme manner as evidenced by the recent flood events.

The Periyar Project undoubtedly puts the wellbeing of the community at great advantage in the Vaigai Valley and could enable a strategy that puts water and power security as a priority

---

[12] Ageing Water Storage Infrastructure: An Emerging Global Risk. UN Report dated 2021

for a region where agricultural demands are increasing and self-sufficiency of food supply vital for the future. The region may also become an important laboratory for biodiversity in the tropics.

On the other hand, the Periyar River valley is vulnerable to inundation if the dam were to fail putting the lives of many people at risk. But this is a situation that will have to be ameliorated at some stage in the future.

Nonetheless, with the desperate need to generate green energy to underpin the strategy there are opportunities for augmenting existing hydroelectric power. The considerable surface area of the reservoir and the distributed tanks provide the opportunity for floating solar energy generation on a very large scale.

The approach for the future of the Periyar Project should take account of the attitude of John Pennycuick and his engineers. Knowledge about the local Natural History, engineering and agricultural practices rather than any conquering mindset enabled the British engineers to go forth with the project. As evident from the plentiful writing in colonial reports, the British had understood that no alternatives existed other than bringing water from a different basin from the Western Ghats. Hence they embarked upon a project to build a dam across the river Periyar - an idea of the indigenous people. All the environmental hazards were well understood from the planning stage and the project was executed causing minimal harm to the local environment.

CAMEO OF A LEADER – JOHN PENNYCUICK

Figure 34. John Pennycuick probably taken in 1870

John Pennycuick – Record and Reputation

The entry for John Pennycuick in Who was Who in India (2004) shows that he spent 34 years in the Public Works Department, Madras, of which he was the Head for five and a half years. No mention is made of his leadership of the Periyar Dam Project for which he is well known and celebrated in southern India, particularly in the state of Tamil Nadu. There is, however, mention of his dedication to cricket and "that he contributed largely to the development of the game in India". Whilst he did indeed leave a legacy of cricketing prowess, his greater achievement, in the minds of countless citizens of India, is the agricultural prosperity that he brought to Tamil Nadu through the Periyar Project.

So strong is this association with John Pennycuick and the Periyar Dam in the State of Tamil Nadu that a granite bust and plinth were flown from India to be placed by his grave in St Peter's Church, Frimley in 2018. This tribute was made after his burial place became common knowledge to the Tamil community one hundred and seven years after his death in 1911. During this time, though, there have been many tributes to him in India, both formal and familial. As well as statues, his distinctive Victorian moustachioed profile can be seen on the advertising hoardings of market gardens on the roadside between Madurai and Thekkady, the area that owes most to his legacy.

Subsequently the Minister for Tamil Nadu, Mr M K Stalin, has dedicated a bust of John Pennycuick to the town of Camberley where he retired to become a local Councillor. The bust was recognised by the MP for Surrey Heath which includes Camberley, the Rt Hon Dr Al Pinkerton who made particular reference to the legacy of John Pennycuick in his maiden speech in the House of Commons in July 2024.

Family background and Early Life in India

Born in Poona on 15th January 1841, John Pennycuick was the product of a military family deeply involved in the East India Company's military campaigns. When he had reached the impressionable age of eight years old, his brother Alick was killed whilst defending the body of his father, Brig Gen John Pennycuick CB KH at the battle of Chillianwala in 1849 during the second Anglo-Sikh war.

John Pennycuick's sense of fortitude and resolve may have been learned from his mother's response to this family catastrophe. She returned home to England with her remaining nine children. In straitened circumstances, she established a new life and arranged for John Pennycuick to attend Cheltenham College, an institution providing schooling to children of British soldiers who had died in battle. John Pennycuick's education at Cheltenham College and Christ's Hospital gave him a moral and Christian foundation that seemed to run through his character for life and imbued him with a strong sense of purpose born, perhaps, of a sense of Christian zeal imparted by his school environment.

Education

He demonstrated intelligence and application at Cheltenham College to gain a place at Addiscombe Military College providing a military grounding and education in the "sciences of Mathematics, Fortification, Natural Philosophy, and Chemistry; the Hindustani,

Latin, and French languages". This broad education, that encouraged technical initiative, was to stand John Pennycuick in good stead for finding innovative solutions to difficult engineering problems. He was commissioned into the Indian Engineers in 1858 (later to become a Royal Engineer after the transition of the government of India to the Crown) and posted to Madras in 1860 to the Madras Engineer Group as an Engineer Army Officer.

India Posting

The India that he had left with his mother and siblings only 10 years previously had changed profoundly. The Sepoy Rebellion of 1858 took place whilst John Pennycuick was attending Addiscombe Military College, had been resolved by the time he was posted to India. By 1860 the facade of British Rule was securely in place again, but with a fundamentally different way of governing. With the rebellion crushed, and the final abolition of the East India Company, British territories in south Asia were now formally governed by the British Crown, but with a more inclusive approach. The Indian Civil Service (ICS) had been established and there were many more career opportunities for local people. Institutions for development of Indian expertise had been established as centres of excellence for the ICS in both India and Britain. John Pennycuick was to become president of the Royal Indian Engineering College, Cooper's Hill, after his return to England, furthering the ambitions of young Indian engineers until his retirement in 1899.

John Pennycuick joined the Madras Engineer Group, informally known as the Madras Sappers, an engineer group of the Corps of Engineers of the Indian Army. The Madras Sappers draw their origin from the erstwhile Madras Presidency army of the British Raj with its HQ in Bengaluru. The Madras Sappers, the oldest of the three groups of the Corps of Engineers in India, survived, unscathed in structure and reputation, following the extensive reorganisations that took place after 1862. The Madras Engineer Group had a large area of operations covering southern India, and John Pennycuick reported to the Madras operational headquarters.

The Abyssinia Campaign

In 1868, junior officer John Pennycuick was deployed with the Madras Sappers and Miners to Abyssinia in a campaign commanded by a late Engineer officer, Lt-Gen Robert Napier, also a graduate of Addiscombe College.

John Pennycuick was appointed to command H Company in a campaign that developed railways and roads in country. The Royal Engineers built a road into the interior to assist the army move supplies quickly over long distances. Timing was an important factor, as the campaign needed to be completed before the torrential June rains made difficult terrain impassable. The Army had to cover 400 miles from Zula on the Red Sea Coast to Magdala where the citadel was stormed to rescue hostages taken by the Ethiopian Emperor Theodore. John Pennycuick was mentioned in despatches as a result of his leadership of the advance to Magdala.

The engineer-led campaign was noted for technical innovations to keep the army moving and supplied in remote areas, including the development of telegraph and desalination plants to turn sea water into fresh water. John Pennycuick would have been in the thick of an operation which was logistically self-sufficient for the first time in history, establishing supply-lines in country.

There is no doubt that John Pennycuick would have gained leadership experience of the operational deployment of transport and logistics which are reflected in his later leadership of the Periyar Project. The skills he learned in the Abyssinia Campaign, including railway construction and road building in mountainous terrain, contributed to the innovative approach he demonstrated after he had arrived back in India.

Family Life

John Pennycuick married Georgina Grace Chamier on the 16th of December 1879 and she had five daughters over the following ten years. Grace was the daughter of Lieutenant General Chamier CB RA and a significant catch, so John Pennycuick was bound to have improved his military profile and his influence within the Madras Engineer Group.

Figure 35. Grace Pennycuick

Quite how the Pennycuicks sustained a family way of life in the brutal and isolating conditions of the Western Ghats of southern India is a matter of great wonder and admiration. But

Grace appears in all the milestone-event photographs by her husband, always elegant and a picture of confidence. She must have resided for some of the time in the bungalow overlooking the nascent main dam. At other times, probably the fever season, she may have stayed at a bungalow featured in photographs near Kodakanal some 30 miles distant. The location was a Hill Station where staff were sent for rest and recuperation. Whilst she may have been accustomed to the way of life in India, the fact that she gave birth to five children between 1880 and 1889 in such basic conditions is a tribute to her strength and stamina.

John Pennycuick was engaged in the most difficult years of the construction of the main dam, watershed cutting and the tunnel whilst his daughters were under the age of ten, which must have placed the burden of upbringing and schooling on Grace in a way that is difficult to comprehend in this time. Her self-sufficiency was to serve her well during her time as a mother in India and after the family returned to England in 1896.

John Pennycuick retired after the opening of the dam. The Madras Cricket Club gave him a farewell party. He returned to Britain in 1896 with his wife and five daughters, and took up the post of president of the Royal Indian Engineering College, Cooper's Hill, from which he resigned in 1899. He was invited to Australia to give advice on the flooding of the Brisbane river the same year, which he undertook with professionalism.

Even though his reputation earned him the status of senior adviser on global water control, his entry in Who Was Who did not mention his acclaimed project:

"COL. JOHN PENNYCUICK, C.S.I., who died at Camberley on March 9th, was born on January 15, 1841, at Poona. He did not obtain his colours at Cheltenham, but in India, where the greater part of his life was spent, he did much for the game, especially in promoting and encouraging it among the natives. In all matches during his career he scored over 12,000 runs and took considerably over 2,000 wickets."

Character of A Leader

The character of John Pennycuick is clear from his deeds, but more significantly from his leadership. A leader with deep understanding of the Indian famine tragedy. A visionary with an appreciation of the grand strategy for harnessing the power of nature. A planner using all the innovations of his age to manage a giant enterprise. A man of action to drive forward progress on the Periyar Project against all odds. A finisher who saw the job through to the end.

Two distinguishing aspects of his character mark him out as a leader of great stature. First, his willingness to take risk in the face of authority. John Pennycuick resolutely designed and implemented the vents that controlled the flow of water through the dam in defiance of authority. Secondly, his great foresight in realising and enabling great engineering opportunities. He enabled the conditions necessary for hydroelectric power half a century before it was implemented. These lessons of leadership provide an example for modern day engineers as they tackle the issues of climate change.

But the greatest legacy of John Pennycuick is the reservoir of human regard in Tamil Nadu for his numerous deeds that brought about an agricultural and subsequent economic revolution in the Vaigai valley. Surely this deep affection must be an abiding lesson for so many aspects of our current way of life? The need to share technology and apply solutions where they benefit humanity most; the need to operate collaboratively down to the lowest level of command; the need to behave reciprocally to develop skills and knowledge; the need to develop understanding about the people of other communities and especially those of our Commonwealth of diverse nations.

We should therefore cherish and promote the abiding affection held by the population of Tamil Nadu for John Pennycuick and give partnership every opportunity to flourish.©

Figure 36. Author at Memorial for John Pennycuick at Lower Camp

"Colonel John Pennycuick has left in Madras an honoured name and has bequeathed a heritage of exalted ideals which should never be suffered to decline". Preface to The Periyar Project by A T Mackenzie. London 22nd April 1898.

Figure 37. The bust of John Pennycuick in the Memorial Gardens, St Peter's Church, Frimley Parish presented by Dr. A. K. Viswanathan, IPS 2018

Figure 38. Bust of John Pennycuick presented by the Chief Minister of Tamil Nadu: M K Stalin

Bibliography

Supplement to The Engineer July 15th 1892. Lake Vrynwy and the Vrynwy Water Supply to Liverpool.

Sanghera, Sathnam, Empireland. Penguin. 2021.

Mackenzie, AT, History of the Periyar Project. Government of Madras, 1963.

Vijaypadma G Mullaiperiyar Dam – A brief History. A compilation.

Minutes of Proceedings of the Institution of Civil Engineers VOL CXXVIII "The Diversion of the Periyar"

Seenivasan,R, Historical Validity of Mullaperiyar Project. Economic and Political Weekly , JANUARY 25, 2014, Vol. 49,

Ageing Water Storage Infrastructure: An Emerging Global Risk. UN Report dated 2021

Nelson JH, The Madura Country. 1868.

Amrith, Sunil, Unruly Waters. Penguin 2018.

Boulton Marshal M Agrarian Radicalism in South India. Princeton University Press 1985.

Ganesh A Water Resources, Evaluation Methods and Techniques. Satish Serial Publishing House 2006.

Tirtha, Ranjit, Geography of India. Prem Rawat for Rawat Publications. New Delhi 1996.

Bayly, CA. Indian Society and the Making of the British Empire. CUP, Cambridge 2010

www.ingramcontent.com/pod-product-compliance
Lightning Source LLC
LaVergne TN
LVHW070939070526
838199LV00039B/722